The Real West

The Real West

Michael Johnson

First published in 1983 by
Octopus Books Limited
59 Grosvenor Street London W1

© 1983 Hennerwood Publications Limited

ISBN 0 86273 073 2

Produced by Mandarin Publishers Limited
22a Westlands Road Quarry Bay Hong Kong

Printed in Hong Kong

ENDPAPERS Louis Maurer, *Buffalo Bill
Hunting Indians* (*c.* 1885).
HALF-TITLE PAGE William T. Ranney,
A Trapper Crossing the Mountains (*c.* 1853).
TITLE SPREAD Thomas Otter, *On the Road* (1860).
PAGES 4 AND 5 Emanuel Leutze, *Westward
the Course of Empire Takes Its Way* (1861).

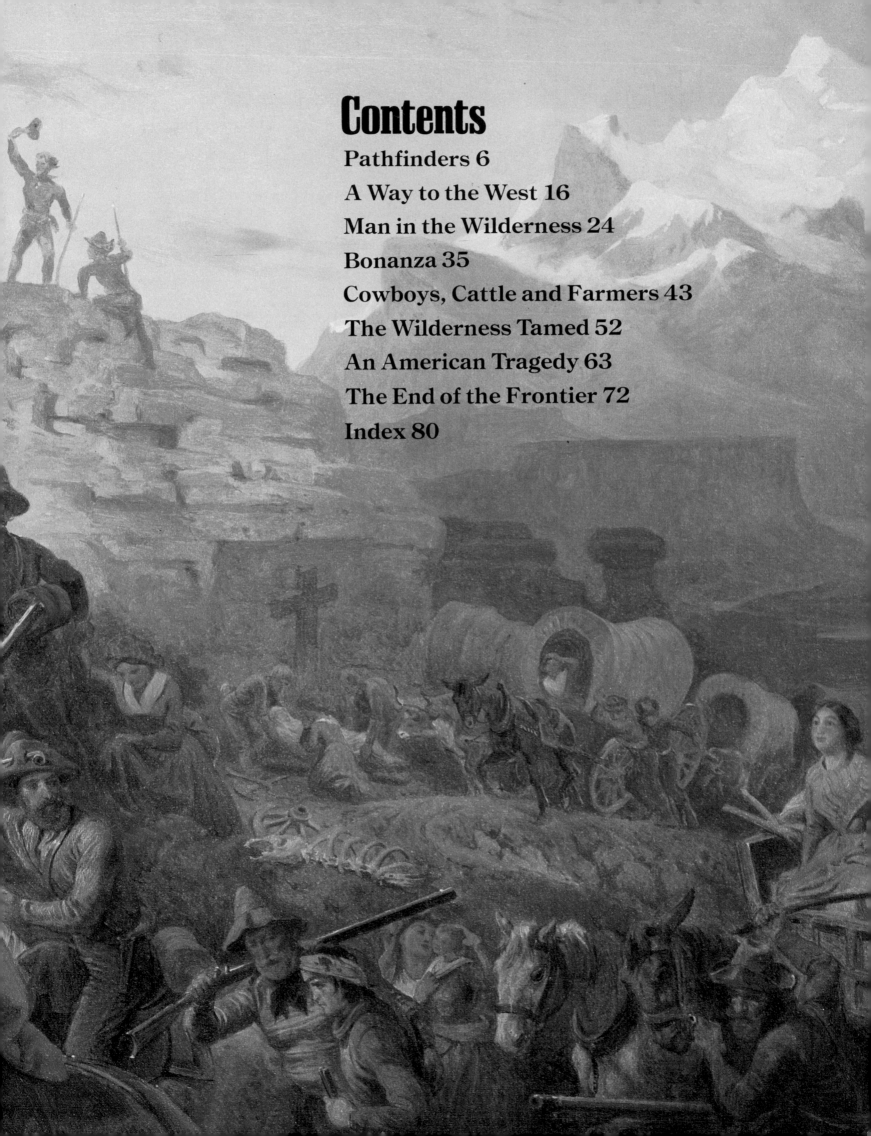

Contents

Pathfinders

*In 1803 the infant United States acquired vast
territories to the west of the Mississippi.
The Louisiana Purchase opened the way
for the last and greatest episode in a
westward movement that had begun more
than 100 years before....*

In the spring of 1799 Daniel Boone, the great pioneer of the American backwoods, chopped down a yellow poplar and began to make an 18 m (60 ft) canoe. Swindled out of his landholdings in Kentucky and worried by creditors, he was preparing to move on. 'Old woman,' he told his wife, 'we must move, for now they are crowding us.' In September he packed up family and goods, and set off down the Ohio river, abandoning the Kentucky landscape which, for 30 years, he had tamed and fought for and moulded. Some 1000 km (600 miles) to the west lay the frontier, where the great brown line of the Mississippi divided the infant United States from the French and Spanish territories to the West. The old patriarch Boone took that direction, striding along the riverbank to keep pace with his family flotilla, and walking every inch of the way. He was 65 and heading to a new life in the West.

For Boone this was nothing new: almost all of his adult life he had been following the westward movement. Born in 1734 into a small community of immigrant English Quakers not far from Philadelphia, he had grown up on the edge of the wilderness. From visiting Indians who squatted impassively in his grandfather's farmyard, from trappers and adventurers who brought furs and skins up the Great Valley trading route from the Carolinas, he heard accounts of vistas and limitless opportunities beyond the barrier of the Allegheny mountains. He was to be one of the pathfinders who pioneered a route through the Cumberland Gap, one of the gateways to the interior from the southern Alleghenies. From birth he had one foot in the wild, and at the age of 16 he began the westward trail. Traveller, explorer, surveyor, soldier, hunter, and farmer, he progressed through Virginia, North Carolina, and Tennessee to Kentucky, wrestling with new tracks, new soil, new wilderness. And now, when Kentucky drove him out, he pursued the setting sun once again to the frontier of the new republic.

The pathfinders of the old American colonies, among whom Daniel Boone was pre-eminent, had begun to beat out the routes westward, and the tradition continued with their descendants. A son of Boone was the first American to camp on the site of present-day Denver (Colorado); one of his grandsons was a well-known government agent among the Colorado Indians; the mother of Kit Carson (a famous 'mountain man' and army scout) was also a Boone. In Daniel Boone's last resting place, St Charles, just across the Missouri from St Louis, there is a plaque in front of the courthouse commemorating one of the old man's trails. It claims that this dusty track was the start of the highway to the west; that out of this path grew 'the Santa Fe Trail, the Salt Lake Trail, and the Great Oregon Trail'. There is justice in this claim: by listening so steadily to the call of the West, Boone became a guide to the American future.

Many were the desires of the pioneer heart in North America. Independence, adventure, riches, political and religious freedom: all these were wanted. But nothing was looked for so eagerly as space. The early history of the United States is the story of a free people in search of free land. It is the story of a westward migration. By 1800, however, the colonists had only nibbled at the edges of the vast territory, and no one knew its geography, its wealth, or its dangers. As the feet of the pioneers, now liberated from the constricting life of the old east-coast colonies, made tracks towards the Great Plains and the Rocky Mountains, so their imagination took wings. The more the West was desired, the more fabulous it became. The far-distant Rockies, looming ominous and jagged through the blue-grey haze of summer heat, or through the white tatters of a winter snowstorm, were transformed into a mythical haven of all desire. 'Those mountains,' wrote an early, typical enthusiast, 'surpass anything of the kind in other quarters of the world. In future ages they may be found to contain more riches in their bowels than those of Indostan and Malibar.' That was not all. They were also the gateway to the land that would give rest to every weary spirit. 'To the west of these mountains may be found lakes, rivers, and countries, full fraught with all the necessaries and luxuries of life; and where future generations may find asylum.' Prophecy was heaped on speculation, until no one knew what to believe. Only the Indians had travelled there.

If, in the year 1800, lack of information was one bar to western travel, another far more serious block in the path of American expansion was the huge tract of foreign territory that stood between the United States and the Western Sea (Pacific). The American colonies were confined to the region east of the Mississippi river, and especially to the eastern seaboard. In the middle of the continent was the French Louisiana Territory, consisting of all the land drained by the Mississippi to the west of the river and covering nearly all the central plains as far as the Rockies. To the south-west was Spanish land, made up of California, Texas, and Mexico, which had been settled and administered by Spain for more than two centuries. And in the north-west, between the Rockies and the Western Sea, was the Oregon country, rain-swept and mountainous, a haunt of fur traders but without settlements; this was disputed land to which both America and England laid claim.

When Thomas Jefferson was inaugurated president in 1801, no one saw the obstacles to American expansion more clearly than he; and no one was more determined or better able to deal with them. Jefferson, more than any of his revolutionary countrymen, had the keenest vision for the future of the young republic. A few years before, in 1796, a French report on Louisiana had stated that 'when

OPPOSITE At the beginning of the 19th century Americans liked to imagine the unexplored West as a paradise of unsurpassed beauty. Later, many artists helped to encourage this image – none more so than Albert Bierstadt, whose enormous *Domes of the Yosemite* is an over-romantic view of a now-famous valley in California's Sierra Nevada.

two nations possess, one the coast and the other the plains, the former must inevitably strike out or submit'. Jefferson felt the truth of this judgment, and he did not intend to submit. He meant to strike out, for he knew that the French report was also right when it said that North America must 'form in the future one single compact nation'.

Fortunately for Jefferson, events in Europe worked to help him. In 1762 France had ceded the Louisiana Territory to Spain. By 1800 Napoleon had won it back, although Spanish influence was still strong in the southern Mississippi valley. And now Napoleon intended to use this land as a springboard for his imperial and anti-English plans in the New World. But his ventures in the Americas began to go wrong. His soldiers went down to yellow fever in San Domingo; his treasury was drained; his bitter struggle against England forced him to concentrate his resources in Europe. With a sudden decision that only dictators can achieve, Napoleon decided to cut his losses, abandon America, and sell Louisiana to Jefferson, if only to keep it out of English hands.

In the spring of 1803 the American minister in France, who was cautiously negotiating for the purchase of New Orleans, was suddenly offered instead an extraordinary prize: the whole of the Louisiana Territory. Without striking a blow, the young United States overnight doubled its land area. For 23,213,567 dollars Jefferson gained 2,145,000 km² (828,000 sq miles), at just over 4 cents an acre. It was one of the best bargains in the history of international commerce.

A Route to the Pacific

Now the way to the far west was open, but the stumbling block of ignorance still remained. Where were the paths? Who was to be the guide? Jefferson had foreseen this problem too, and even before the Louisiana Purchase, in 1801, he had ordered his private secretary, Capt Meriwether Lewis, to prepare for an expedition that would blaze a trail to the headwaters of the Missouri, across the Rockies, and then down to the Pacific, using the lower waters of the Columbia river.

Lewis prepared carefully. Already an experienced woodsman, he studied zoology, botany, and celestial navigation. And to offset his own bookish, moody nature, he chose a former colleague to be his co-leader. This was Capt William Clark, a genial redhead who got on with everyone, soldiers and Indians alike. He was a practical fellow, good with his hands, full of common sense and ingenuity. He was also a master of rivercraft and a daring boatman. He found the wilderness an exciting challenge, and he could fire his men with the same excitement. These two young men together were a rare combination of intelligence and skill, of practical ability and science. They were ideal commanders.

In the late 18th century Daniel Boone helped to pioneer routes westwards through the Allegheny range. In this famous painting by George Caleb Bingham he is seen escorting settlers through Cumberland Gap. From this pass the way west was clear through Tennessee and Kentucky to the Mississippi and beyond.

For the body of his expedition, Lewis wanted, and got, 'good hunters, stout, healthy, unmarried men, accustomed to the woods, and capable of bearing bodily fatigue in a pretty considerable degree.' He chose nine Kentucky woodsmen and a tough crew of 14 volunteer U.S. soldiers. He then added two French boatmen and a French half-breed hunter who was also interpreter, tracker, and guide. With Clark went his black servant York, and Lewis took his large Newfoundland dog Scannon. Their boats for the Missouri were a 17 m (55 ft) keelboat (a shallow craft, pointed at both ends), with square sail and 22 oars, and two light pirogues (large dugouts). Through the winter of 1803-4 the expedition prepared and trained in camp on the east bank of the Mississippi, while Lewis was in nearby St Louis gleaning information and hiring extra French *voyageurs* (fur-company boatmen) to help with the first leg of the journey into Indian country. On 14 May 1804, a rainy Monday, the expedition set out.

The Missouri of the great plains was not unknown. French traders and *voyageurs* were familiar with the river valley and the Indians who lived there; and Lewis had taken trouble to collect this knowledge, getting hold of the best maps and the best advice. But as the clumsy keelboat swung north-westward into the mouth of the Missouri, and bucked under the weight of the vast, brown, rain-swollen spring waters of 'Big Muddy', even the bravest of the travellers must have felt momentarily overwhelmed by feelings of strangeness and danger.

The river was treacherous and ever-changing, swinging in wide loops. The current was strong and unpredictable, biting into the soft shores, swirling over sandbanks and hidden snags, rushing at islands that seemed to block all passage, so that the main channel was almost impossible to identify. Winds abruptly changed direction, the storms were sudden and violent. The square sail of the keelboat was useless in these conditions. Oars were useful in slack water, but too often progress was achieved against the current only by exhausting work on the tow-lines, the strained ropes scouring neck and back muscles. The men were as much in the river as in the boats, sinking thigh deep into a glutinous clay. For those on the bank there was no path. The underbrush was thick and ungiving. Trees and debris brought down by flood tangled with shore

In his journal of the Lewis and Clark expedition, Capt Meriwether Lewis made detailed notes and sketches of everything of interest. These two pages include a sketch map of the course of the Missouri in the area of Fort Mandan, where the explorers wintered in 1804.

vegetation, and in many places only heavy work with axe and machete could force a way through.

The summer heat was fierce. Snakes and ticks and a million biting insects made life hellish. Worst of all were the ever-present mosquitoes. Naked, toiling men scratched their bodies raw, so that blood and grime and sweat covered them like a warpaint. In the woods, the hunters lost their aim as a mass of black insects danced before their eyes. And at night there was no rest, so men woke still exhausted. 'I am very Sick,' complained the young sergeant Charles Floyd to his dairy, 'and Has been for Sometime.' Within three weeks he was dead.

Laboriously, the expedition averaged a respectable 14.5 km (9 miles) a day. Clark, the talented waterman, was generally in the boats, while Lewis plodded along the bank, hunting or making notes and observations. They kept a stern eye on the men, and both dispassionately record the floggings: in May, 50 lashes to Collins for disobeying orders; in June, 50 lashes to Hall for stealing whiskey and 100 to Collins (again!) for being drunk on post; in July, 100 to Willard for sleeping on guard. Nor did these punishments disrupt the good spirit of the party: the men were not milksops, and knew from experience how much discipline was needed in strange Indian country.

July saw them reach the sandy mouth of the Platte. They celebrated the 4th (Independence Day) with a salute on the swivel guns of the keelboat and an extra ration of whiskey. In August came the first close contact with Indians, at a place the travellers called Council Bluffs (Iowa). Meeting a party of Yankton Sioux, the captains anchored on a sandbank, set out an awning and whiskey, and negotiated a friendly agreement which the Indians had neither the intention nor the power to keep. But a month later, coming upon some Teton Sioux at Bad River (South Dakota) on 24 September, the captains knew that these aggressive, piratical relatives of the Yankton meant trouble (the great warrior Sitting Bull would be born into the Tetons' Hunkpapa tribe in 1834).

Lewis had been warned by the *voyageurs* about the Teton Sioux, and he was resolved not to be intimidated. This meeting might be crucial for future Indian relations, so Lewis kept his abrupt temper in check, though sorely tried by 1000 menacing Sioux; he made it known that he would fight if necessary, but would not be stopped. For

A Mandan Indian earth and wicker lodge. In winter these large buildings sheltered horses as well as people. The explorers found the Mandans hospitable; one of their chiefs taught Capt Clark how to kill buffalo with bow and arrow.

After reaching the Pacific Lewis and Clark spent several months exploring the coast and the Columbia estuary, where they had friendly encounters with Indians, including these Chinooks. In Charles M. Russell's watercolour the Indian girl Sacagawea, who acted as interpreter, is in the nearest boat behind Clark's black servant York.

four days Lewis and Clark sweated it out; then suddenly the Indians gave way, and the Americans moved on with a sigh of relief. A month later, peacefully approaching the Mandan villages at Knife River (North Dakota), the expedition felt, in the cold, shortening, late-October days, the oncoming of winter. A little below the first village, in a river bottom on the east bank, they built a snug post of cottonwood logs, and got ready to winter in this place they called Fort Mandan.

Fort Mandan stood at a crossroads of frontier travel. Traders came up the river from the south; from northern lands came the fur trappers of the Canadian Hudson's Bay and North West companies. Although isolated, the little fort was lively enough that winter. Wanderers arrived from Indian country and were keenly questioned. One, an aged trader named Toussaint Charbonneau, was added

to the expedition – mainly because his wife, Sacagawea (a 16-year-old Shoshone girl, pregnant and ill), was likely to be useful as an interpreter, and perhaps as a guarantee of safe passage, among the Indians of the north-west.

In February 1805, helped by rattlesnake medicine, Sacagawea painfully gave birth to a boy, Baptiste, whom Clark nicknamed Pomp. By March the river was clearing, and the wild geese winged north-east. On 7 April, having returned the keelboat to St Louis with several men, Lewis started again on his 'darling project'. Now the real work of discovery began. With six small canoes and two pirogues, 'we were about to penetrate a country at least 2000 miles in width, on which the foot of civilized man had never trodden; the good or evil it had in store for us was for experiment yet to determine...'.

The Missouri swung west, into the lonely, eroded terrain of the North Dakota Badlands. Keen winds blew across this wilderness and the nights were nipped by frost. Game was plentiful, and bison, elk, wolves, and bears roamed undisturbed. Grizzlies were a formidable danger. The hunter George Drouillard needed 10 shots to kill one monster, which measured over 2.6 m (8½ ft) high and almost 1.8 m (6 ft) around the chest. In rising country navigation was difficult, the Missouri and its tributaries (including hereabouts the mighty Yellowstone) running into each other indistinctly. At the Marias river (in central Montana) the captains cached a part of the stores in order to travel more lightly, for they expected soon to begin the portage (carrying the boats) across the Rockies.

Over the Rockies

On 13 June Lewis saw the spray and the mists of the Great Falls, of which the travellers had heard stories from the Indians. Lewis was ill at this time, purging himself with black herb tea, and he could not find Indians to sell him horses for the portage around the falls. The detour took a month of exceptional hardship. Back on the river, they struggled wearily into the foothills of the Rockies, and came to a puzzling three-way fork – the Missouri branching into what the travellers named the Jefferson, Madison, and Gallatin rivers. After more wasted time, Clark limped off with boils and swollen feet to follow the course of the westward-flowing Jefferson. The rest dragged behind him, 'sick with high fever and very fatigued', climbing beside the diminishing current to what is now regarded as the source of the Missouri. On 12 August, a soldier stood with a foot on either bank of the little outflow: the mighty river had been conquered.

Leaving the river and struggling over a pass into the Lemhi valley (Idaho), the party now needed horses badly. Few Indians had been seen, and those only in the distance. At last, luck brought them to a wretched, starving band of Shoshone, who became friendly and agreed to provide a few horses only when Sacagawea recognized the chief, Cameahwait, as her brother. Then, armed with Indian advice on how best to negotiate the mountains, they pushed into Bitterroot valley. Storms sent landslips, and the horses crashed off the narrow trail. It was September, and the snows were beginning to block the high passes. They lived for days on berries and wolf-meat; then they were reduced to candles and bear-oil. Later they ate dog, and did not dislike it. 'We suffered everything,' Clark wrote, 'which hunger, cold and fatigue could impose.' Under flying snow, a very miserable band of Americans, shaky with dysentery, crossed over the Bitterroot mountains via the Lolo Pass, and staggered at last into a Nez Percé village on the Clearwater river.

They had passed over the Great Divide, and were now beyond the most distant frontier of the former Louisiana Territory. They were, moreover, on a navigable river system which would take them down to the Western Sea: the Clearwater flows into the Snake, which is a tributary of the Columbia. So the captains ordered pines to be felled and dugouts made. The descent, they were warned, was tricky, with many cataracts and falls. But winter was pressing close: with daring haste they plunged down the rivers, running cataracts with a recklessness that amazed the Indians. On 22 October, the Celilo Falls on the Columbia, where the boiling river roars into a 46 m (150 ft) gorge, forced on them the last major portage. On Thursday, 7 November 1805, beneath a low, rain-scoured sky, they glimpsed the Pacific. 'Ocean in view,' noted an exultant William Clark: 'O! the joy'. They built Fort Clatsop on a tributary of the Columbia and explored the estuary area for five months before starting on their journey home.

Oregon City on the Willamette, which flows northward into the Columbia estuary, was founded in the 1820s by retired employees of the Hudson's Bay Company. This sketch was made in 1845 by Capt Henry Warre, who was hired by the British to report on American activity in the Oregon County, which was then a disputed territory.

Pike in the South-West

Zebulon Pike is brought by his Spanish captors to Santa Fe in the spring of 1807. Pike's mission had been to explore the ill-defined frontier between the Spanish south-west and the territory acquired by the United States in the Louisiana Purchase.

Even while Lewis and Clark were so brilliantly carrying out the president's plans, Jefferson was preparing other expeditions. The unexplored area of the Louisiana Territory was so vast, who knew where the best lands and the best paths might lie? Several large east-west valleys south of the Missouri – notably of the Arkansas, Canadian, and Red rivers – pointed attractively towards the Rockies, and a couple of minor scientific surveys had had encouraging results. In 1806 Lt Zebulon Pike, having won his explorer's spurs on a modest adventure up the Mississippi, was ready to tackle the dry lands of the Arkansas and the Red rivers in Kansas and Oklahoma. Part of Pike's brief was to 'test' the frontier between the United States' newly acquired territory and the Spanish south-west.

On 15 July Pike started out with a small party towards Pawnee country in what is now western Kansas. Here he met a hostile reception, for the

Spaniards had warned the Indians to have nothing to do with the Americans. Pike, a confident 27-year-old, loftily told the chief that 'the warriors of his great American Father were not women, to be turned back by words.' He pushed on – but in the wrong direction; and as winter came on, bringing its familiar hardships, he was still wandering far to the north of the Red river. He tracked westward into the Colorado Rockies and discovered the 4300 m (14,109 ft) Pike's Peak, which was named after him;

but he was losing valuable time. He hurried south, crossing (but failing to identify) several major rivers until, at the end of winter, he stumbled upon the waters of the Rio Grande.

On the river he built a fort, but soon a company of Spanish horsemen arrived, let him know forcibly that he was in Spanish territory, and took Pike and his party in custody to their northern capital Santa Fe (New Mexico). After a long, circuitous march under guard through New Mexico and Texas, Pike was left at the American border (on the Red river, south of present-day Shreveport, Louisiana).

Within a few years the war of 1812 against the British brought a temporary halt to American ex-

Map showing the routes of the Lewis and Clark and Pike expeditions.

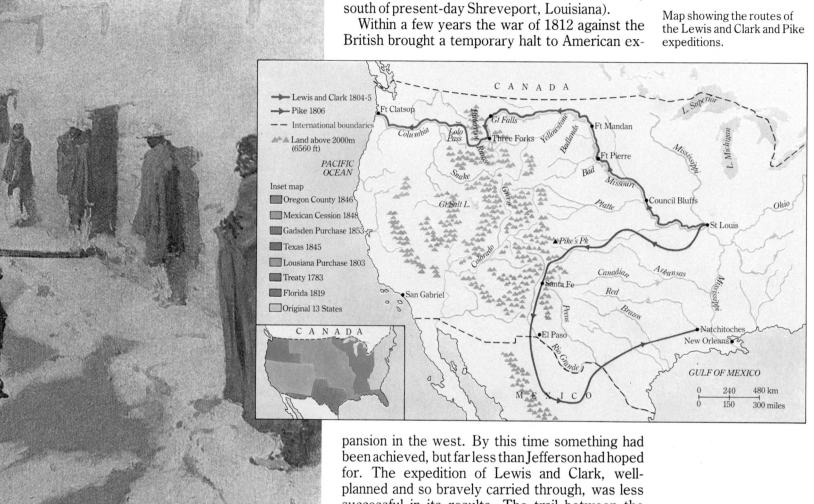

pansion in the west. By this time something had been achieved, but far less than Jefferson had hoped for. The expedition of Lewis and Clark, well-planned and so bravely carried through, was less successful in its results. The trail between the Missouri and the Columbia rivers, which Jefferson had thought might be short and easy, was in fact a 355 km (220-mile) crossing of exceptionally tough country. In the south, the first part of Pike's increasingly muddled journey had shown a way up the Arkansas and Canadian rivers in Oklahoma. But Pike insisted that the central plains to the south of the Missouri were 'incapable of cultivation'.

The immediate hopes were dashed. In the Louisiana Territory, most of the plains and the huge mass of the Rockies were still largely unexplored. Spain blocked the southerly routes to the far West. A tumbled, rain-drenched mountain landscape made the north a nightmare. Everywhere relations with native Indians were uneasy and unresolved. American eyes still looked westward, but had yet to find the channels that would lead to fulfilment.

A Way to the West

*After Lewis and Clark's expedition, much of the
early exploration of the West was done by
fur trappers – 'mountain men' like
John Colter, Jed Smith and Jim Bridger,
who pioneered many of the routes
through the Rockies . . . .*

Although the government expeditions stumbled on the way to the West, and the scientific explorers found little reason to continue, the old human desire for riches soon asserted itself and urged a daring new breed of men along the almost abandoned path to discovery. For many years the British fur companies in Canada (notably the Hudson's Bay Company) had taken a good profit out of the northern Rockies. The United States eyed these riches enviously, and one of the most important tasks given to Lewis and Clark had been to survey 'that productive country of valuable furs exclusively enjoyed at present by the subjects of his Britannic Majesty'. Lewis and Clark had done their work thoroughly,

lot with the trappers, and away he went, back into the high beaver country. He was the first of the American 'mountain men'.

Soon a host of rugged and independent adventurers was on Colter's tail, spurred on by enterprising traders. They poured out of St Louis, which buzzed with rumour and expectations. First away was Manuel Lisa, a villainous-looking Spanish trader. He knew the river well, and intended to set up forts on the streams that led out of the mountains, from which he could supply and maintain the trappers. By 1808 Lisa had organised the Missouri Fur Company and established two trading posts in the foothills.

OPPOSITE Astoria (also known as Fort George) was founded on the southern shore of the Columbia estuary by John Jacob Astor's American Fur Company as its main depot west of the Rockies.

and though they had found the mountains grimly tough and inhospitable, they also had found a great many beavers. The country they went through made communications dangerous and frightened off all but the hardiest settlers, but it soon became a magnet for fur trappers.

On 12 August 1806, returning from the Pacific with Lewis and Clark, the Kentucky woodsman John Colter got talking with two Illinois trappers he met by chance on the upper Missouri. The men were not doing well and were desperate for furs. Colter had now crossed the Rockies twice and knew where the beavers lived. He decided to throw in his

The good prospects also attracted larger fish than Lisa. John Jacob Astor, well on his way to becoming a millionaire, quickly saw an opportunity in the Oregon country. Between 1808 and 1810 he formed two fur companies, sent a ship from New York round Cape Horn to found a trading post at Astoria, near the mouth of the Columbia river, and then followed this up by sending a land party to Astoria in the tracks of the Lewis and Clark expedition in order to secure a trail for the passage of goods and produce.

Within 10 years all these ventures had failed. Lisa's men were driven out by angry Blackfeet and

ABOVE Where possible trappers used boats to transport their heavy loads of beaver pelts to the fur-trading posts. George Caleb Bingham's *Fur Traders Descending the Missouri* (1845) captures the atmosphere of the calm, turbid Big Muddy on a warm summer evening.

Many trappers had violent encounters with Indians, who feared that over-hunting by the fur companies would exterminate the beaver. Charles Deas' *Death Struggle,* painted about 1845, shows the dramatic climax of just such an encounter.

Arikara Indians. The Astorians who went by land explored new country but were as unsuccessful as Lewis and Clark had been in finding a reliably safe mountain trail. And on the Pacific coast, the Astorians on the Columbia surrendered their post to the British during the war of 1812.

Geography, politics and warfare caused these attempts to fail. But the beavers were still there, in abundance all over the Rockies, and the mountain men were still eager to catch them. Lisa's company regrouped, spread further south and, in 1821, under the leadership of General William H. Ashley, formed the Rocky Mountain Company. Astor also abandoned the northern Oregon territory. He based his American Fur Company at St Louis and competed with Ashley in the safer, more southerly land. Driven on by ambitious traders, who either employed the trappers directly or bought the pelts from private individuals, the mountain men took their tools and traps and lean horses deeper and deeper into unknown country. For a life of hardship and the chance of a savage death, they gained the poorest of livings. The profits went to the fur companies; the trappers remained in debt. But time has rewarded them with the gift of fame. It was their persevering and blistered feet that opened the gates of the Rockies.

The Trapper's Life

A friend described John Colter as a man made 'for the hardy endurance of fatigue, privation, and peril'. Very often that was the sum total of the trapper's life. 'If God will only forgive me this time,' Colter vowed after a terrifying encounter with Indians, 'I will leave the country – and be damned if I ever come again'. Broken by the Indians, Colter did get away. But many others, debt-ridden and semi-savage, laboured on to harrowing deaths through being starved, crushed by snowfall or landslip, or killed by Indians or grizzly bears. In official eyes the white trappers were law-breakers, trespassing on Indian rights. The Indians did not understand the white man's greed for beaver skins, and would not gather enough of them, and so the trappers pushed on. They became outlaws, beyond the bounds of society. Their lives and their business were unregulated, always on the edge of disaster. In isolation and poverty, the mountain man pulled his frayed buckskin and tattered furs around him and slipped into the wilderness. There he became at one with the mountains and the beasts.

The first trading posts, where the supplies had been distributed and the skins collected, had been swept away, with serious loss of life, by the Blackfeet and the Arikaras. After 1822 General Ashley worked out a new system of supply. Each year he nominated a completely different rendezvous in some safe valley or secluded meadow, and to this spot at the appointed date swarmed the fur-company men, the trappers with their year's haul of pelts, and any friendly Indians who wished to trade.

In early summer, before the heat withered the land, long pack-trains of mules and horses wound up the valleys of the eastward-flowing rivers and into the foothills, heading for the rendezvous. There they could equip themselves with all that their trade required. For the mountain men there were iron traps; new horses; guns both smooth-bore and rifled, powder and shot; knives, axes, tools, blankets, clothes and boots; tobacco at a dollar a pound, straight alcohol at 5 dollars a pint; also sugar, coffee, flour, and the little luxuries that sweetened the desolation of mountain life. These were the important goods, but the pack-animals carried also the items of Indian trade: glass beads in blue and red and white; mackinaw capes and blankets; scarlet coats for the chiefs; hatchets, files, and fish-hooks; mirrors and feathers and paints, and other gaudy trifles; and of course the whiskey to induce despair and drunkenness, and the tobacco to smoke in the calumet or ceremonial pipe.

Exchanging his year's catch of hard-won pelts for goods that barely kept him alive, the mountain man was off again, trudging steadily towards the loneliness of the high peaks. In this land, the dangers were real. The Indians, badly deceived by the white man, could never be trusted completely; and when they attacked, they were cunning and merciless. Ashley's company lost 20 men in 1823 alone. Four trappers with Andrew Henry were killed by Blackfeet on the upper Missouri. Hurrying to the rescue, General Ashley himself was encircled and attacked by Arikaras, and 14 of his party were killed. Then in August, when Henry was trapping in the Yellowstone valley, his horses were stolen and two more men killed.

Death sometimes seemed a better bargain than capture by Indians. The suffering of John Colter remained as a warning. In 1808, returning with their furs to the Three Forks trading post (at the junction of the Jefferson, Madison, and Gallatin tributaries of the Missouri in present-day Montana), Colter and a companion were surprised by Blackfeet. The companion, John Potts, was killed and mutilated. Colter was stripped naked and given the chance to run for his life. Young and fit, he took his chance, racing over the scrub, lacerating his bare feet on rock and cactus. In his stress, blood spurted from his nose and mouth. Heading for the Madison river he outdistanced all but one of his pursuers, but was able to turn and kill this Indian with his own spear. Still his pursuers tracked him. At the river, Colter dived and surfaced beneath a log-jam, lying quiet in the icy water while his tormentors viciously jabbed at the logs above him. In the freezing night he emerged and fled, climbing a cliff, and running naked for mile upon mile. After 11 days, eating roots and grubs and bark, burnt by day and frozen at night, and with feet beaten to a bloody pulp, he arrived at the safety of a fort on the Bighorn river, more than 320km (200

miles) east of the Madison. Colter kept his vow and retired to a less dangerous life in St Louis.

To add to the danger from Indians, the mountains were also well populated with snakes and cougars and wolves. But most deadly of all were the bears, specially the grizzlies. In 1823 Jedediah Smith, then a new member of the Rocky Mountain Company, was savaged by a grizzly. The bear broke his ribs, partially ripped his scalp from his head, and left one ear hanging from a thread of skin. Coolly, Smith directed one of his companions, James Clyman, to take needle and cotton and sew him together again. 'Then I put in my needle,' the man remembered, 'stitching it through and through, and over and over, laying the lacerated parts together as nice as I could.' Lucky Smith lived and had a famous career as a mountain man; but many others died from bear wounds. In 1824, on his way to New Mexico, James Pattie saw one of his party 'literally torn in pieces': his flesh was slashed, leaving bare sinews; side, throat and face were cleaved open so that 'his breath came through the openings'. Yet somehow this human wreck was still alive, and Pattie, with wilderness all around, had the sad task of making the man comfortable before creeping away and leaving him to die.

In the face of these perils, it is a wonder that men came forward; but come forward they did. When Ashley advertised in St Louis, in 1822, for a hundred 'Enterprising Young Men' to suffer the hardship that the Rocky Mountain Company had to offer, he collected his recruits with ease. No doubt most of them were rough and ready adventurers, strong and self-reliant, but also selfish brawlers and drunkards. They looked to themselves, and to hell with the rest of the world. 'If you see a man's mule running off,' went the typical advice to the tenderfoot, 'don't stop it. Let it go to the devil, it aint yourn. If his sack falls off, don't tell 'im. He'll find out. Help the cook, get wood and water, make yourself active. Then git your pipe and smoke it. Don't be always asking questions, 'an you'll pass.'

But there was another type of man also attracted by Ashley's advertisement. He, too, was a tough adventurer, but he possessed something more. He was curious, and his thirst for knowledge drove him always over the next hill; he took satisfaction in the majesty and the strangeness of the world about him; and he had a sharp mind that could piece together his experience in the wilderness, and turn it to his advantage. He possessed, in fact, the pioneer mind – and he found the West irresistible.

Grizzly bears posed a formidable threat to the mountain men. Jedediah Smith was almost scalped by one in 1823, and in this Currier and Ives print of 1862 the life of a trapper depends on his companion's aim with a rifle.

Mountain Travellers

Two men of this kind who answered Ashley's advertisement were Jedediah Smith and James Bridger, most famous of all mountain men. Jed Smith was quiet, withdrawn, and religious. Among the shaggy ruffians of the hills he was almost a dandy, neat and clean-shaven, and he neither smoked nor drank. Noting daily the cruelty and greed of his fellows, he was pricked by conscience and lamented 'the perverseness of my wicked heart'. He took upon his back the sins of his kind and saw his own hard life as a mission to encourage others: 'to help those who stand in need, I face every danger; it is for this that I traverse the mountains covered with eternal snow.'

But if Smith was the romantic of the Rockies, Jim Bridger was the great realist. Less of a dreamer, perhaps less intelligent than Smith, Bridger, in his 40 years of lonely wandering, came to know the West better than any other American. He also knew and respected the Indians, for he had a succession of three Indian wives. 'There is nothing in his costume or his deportment', wrote an admirer, 'to indicate the heroic spirit that dwells within, simply a plain, unassuming man.'

Hardly ever has such important work of discovery been done by such a surprising group of trailblazers. When John Colter departed from the upper Missouri in 1806 in search of beaver, he had not the slightest awareness that he was being scout and pathfinder for the mighty westward movement to the Pacific. Yet within 50 years, when Jim Bridger had at last hung up his spring-traps and settled on his Kansas farm, nearly every major pass, valley and river in the Rockies had been explored by the mountain men.

The early men did well. Andrew Henry and the Astorians opened many of the trails that Lewis and Clark had found so difficult. Between 1822 and 1828 Ashley's men were as active as the beavers they hunted, making the route from the Mississippi, Missouri, and Platte rivers, through South Pass, and on to the Rockies trapping grounds on the Snake and Green rivers almost as well trodden as a St Louis thoroughfare. In 1824 Bridger discovered the Great Salt Lake (Utah), and in 1825 Ashley navigated part of the Colorado river farther south.

But the boldest of the mountain travellers was Jed Smith. On 22 August 1826 he left the Great Salt Lake with 15 men to explore the unknown South west. After following the Colorado river southwards, he branched west towards California, formerly Spanish but then part of Mexico. In November Smith came to a barren waste. 'I crossed a salt plain,' he wrote of the first American crossing of the Mojave desert; 'on the surface was a crust of beautiful white salt, quite thin.' Entering California by the Cajon Pass, Smith pushed on to the whitewashed adobe (earth and straw) houses of the San Gabriel mission, on the site of modern-day Los

Jim Bridger – a photograph taken in the mid-19th century. With Jed Smith and John Colter he was the most celebrated of the great trail-blazers of the West.

The trappers and pathfinders inspired expeditions by many adventurers, some of whom were ill-equipped for survival in the western wilderness. Alfred Jacob Miller's *The Lost Greenhorn* is based on the adventures of a cook attached to a party led by Sir Drummond Stewart. The young man rode off alone one morning to see if he could track down and kill some buffalo. He was found some days later, half starved and totally lost.

Angeles. Then he went north towards the bay of San Francisco. In the winter, the snows of the Sierra Nevada, where many of his horses died and his men nearly starved, blocked the return to Great Salt Lake; and when he was able to continue he came to the Nevada desert, where 'we frequently travelled without water sometimes for two days.'

In July 1827 Smith was off again from the trappers' rendezvous at Bear Lake (Utah), pursuing unfinished business in California. This time he was not so lucky. Mojave Indians ambushed him and killed 10 men. In California he fell out with the Mexicans, who imprisoned him at Monterey. Freed and ordered out of the territory, he went north, over the Siskiyou Pass and up the coast, to the British fur post of Fort Vancouver on the Columbia. Another great swing inland brought him back to the hunting country of the Teton Sioux.

In the varied wilderness of the Rockies, it was hard to say which was more painful to endure: the winter snows and blizzards of the Oregon country, or the summer sands and burning desert of the south-west. Travellers seemed to find the going more difficult, and the discoveries less rewarding, in the dry south. In 1806 Zebulon Pike had found a harsh trail leading to Santa Fe (New Mexico), and Major Stephen Long, following this route in 1819, agreed with his assessment.

That was bad for settlers, but traders were not so easily put off. They realised that it was shorter from St Louis to Santa Fe than from Santa Fe to the Mexican east coast port of Veracruz. They thought that the northern part of Spanish territory could be provisioned very profitably by Americans, and after Mexico achieved independence from Spain in 1821 trade developed quickly. All kinds of manufactured goods were taken to Santa Fe, and the merchants brought back mules, horses, furs, gold, and silver. By 1824 the Santa Fe Trail was a broad track, suitable for wagons as well as pack-horses.

Santa Fe was merely the threshold to the Southwest. The source of the furs and the gold and the silver lay beyond in the lands of Mexico and California. Jed Smith had blazed a trail from the Great Salt Lake to lower California, but he had gone through grim and dangerous country. Shortly after Smith, two other fur trappers working from Santa Fe pioneered easier, more southerly routes. James Pattie drifted slowly down the Gila river in 1827, then struck west to the Pacific coast at San Diego. Three years later William Wolfskill established the Spanish Trail, swinging north around the ferocious waters of the Grand Canyon on the Colorado, and coming to the coast near present-day Los Angeles.

Gentlemen Explorers

The period 1806 to 1830 was the era of the mountain men. They opened the way. Then, in the years from 1830 to 1850, another kind of explorer was drawn to the West. These were the gentlemen-travellers,

footloose young men of spirit and education who were attracted by frontier adventure. Some were of the type that Alexander Ross had noted, at Astoria in 1811, setting out for a journey by canoe on the Columbia, 'one with a cloak on his arm, another with an umbrella, a third with pamphlets and newspapers for amusement'. The energetic Scotsman Capt William Stewart was a superior example of this type, a sportsman who popped up in the oddest places, puzzling the mountain men but gaining their respect. 'What he wanted out thar in the mountains, I never jest rightly know'd,' said one old-timer. 'He was no trader, nor a trapper, and flung his dollars right smart. Thar was old grit in him too, and a hair of the black b'ar at that.' High praise from a mountain veteran.

Other gentlemen had more complicated motives than Stewart, who was merely out for fun and adventure. From 1832-4 the gallant Capt Benjamin de Bonneville attacked the wilderness by storm. Bonneville was a military man apparently determined to subdue mountain and desert by willpower alone. But apart from some useful mapping by Joseph Walker of the Great Basin desert region, his expeditions accomplished little, apart from building a trading post nicknamed 'Fort Nonsense' on account of its poor position.

Ten years later, the trained surveyor John Charles Frémont achieved much more. He was certainly a gentleman, as his writings clearly showed. He lamented the rough incivility of life in the Rockies: the lack of the comforting inn 'which awaits the tired traveller on his return from Mont Blanc, or the orange groves of South America with their refreshing juices and soft fragrant airs.' But Frémont was very competent, ambitious and energetic, and for 12 years from 1842 he surveyed and mapped large tracts of the central Rockies, the Great Basin, and the Sierra Nevada. In his wanderings, he went from Tucson (Arizona) in the south to Fort Walla Walla (Washington state) in the north, from Fort Laramie (Wyoming) and Pueblo (Colorado) on the eastern margins of the Rockies to Monterey on the Pacific coast.

Frémont was more than a mere surveyor: he was a man with a vision. He had married the daughter of Senator Thomas Benton, the most influential champion among Washington officials of western development. Frémont shared the enthusiasm of his father-in-law. Benton had helped to place him in charge of surveying the West, and from this task both men anticipated a double achievement. They expected a great increase in scientific map-making; but also they hoped to discover the safest and quickest line of 'emigrant travel across the mountains'.

'The Mississippi was never designed as the western boundary of the American Empire,' a confident American geographer had written in 1789. By 1850, time had proved him right. The circle of

the Union was complete. The Oregon Treaty in 1846 had established the border with Canada at the 49th parallel. The victorious end to the war with Mexico in 1848 had brought into the United States the vast acreage of formerly Spanish land in Texas and the South-west. The Great Plains were criss-crossed with trails, the gates through the Rockies had been opened, the surf-scarred Pacific shore was calling to a host of immigrants. And these people, the 'pilgrims' that Fremont and Benton wanted, came in their thousands. A population 'assembled from all the States of the Union and from all the nations of Europe is rushing in like the waters of the flood'.

The movement westward seemed irresistible. Pile the Alleghenies upon the Rockies, a senator from Missouri cried, 'and our people will scale them. The march of empire is westward; nothing

will, nothing can check it'. The pull was felt in the farthest and quietest corners of the eastern states. The writer Henry David Thoreau felt it in his little Massachusetts hut, where he had gone for seclusion by Walden Pond. 'Westward I go free,' he wrote, striding in imagination towards the Rockies. And that, he said, was the direction his countrymen must take. 'I must walk towards Oregon and not towards Europe'. The West was the true American land, the untamed wilderness in which the young nation would test and prove itself.

A land of dreams appeared towards the setting sun, and men rushed to possess it with feverish haste. The shrewd Frenchman Alexis de Tocqueville, watching in 1833 the frantic exodus from the cities and farms of the east coast, commented that the European immigrants to America were racing to the Pacific like an act of providence.

Man in the Wilderness

By the 1830s several major trails across the continent had been established. Urged on alike by government propaganda, land hunger, and a sense of destiny, the pioneer emigrants pulled up roots — and the wagon trains began to roll....

The traveller to the West stepped off the St Louis riverboat at Independence, 240 km (150 miles) up the Missouri, where the Kansas river joined it from the western side. The typical traveller was no philosopher, and in any case he had little time to reflect. It was enough that the 'manifest destiny' of the American nation had pitched him on to the Oregon Trail with few possessions, more hope, and a great ignorance of the path forward. 'He knew not where he was going', wrote a frontier historian, 'but he was on his way, cheerful, optimistic, busy and buoyant'. Imagination made up for lack of knowledge, and the forms he created in his imagination came to haunt him. In his mind, western skies were clearer, the stars brighter, the air more bracing, the rains gentler, and the earth more fruitful. 'Will not man', asked one enthusiast, 'grow to greater perfection under these influences?'

The traveller left the settlements of civilized society and advanced on to the prairie. He saw a vast slab of plain, rising in low waves. It was cut from east to west by broad, sluggish rivers and by many gullies and gravelly stream-beds, parched in summer but cascading in spring with melted snows. This was a country of tall grass, dank, spongy and battered by storms in the early part of the year, then briefly a magic land carpeted with a myriad wild flowers before a high sun washed out the colour and raised lung-clogging dust.

As the plain gradually rose, the grass became shorter and thinner, the climate drier, and drinking water scarce. By now the traveller was following the Platte, a wide, dirty, alkaline, bitter river, so slow that it appeared to lose its way amid quicksands and islands of stunted willow and cotton wood. Disgusted travellers, tired by its sleepy progress, said it was a mile wide, an inch deep, had water that you could chew, and that it was drinkable only if you threw it away and filled the mug with whiskey. This was coyote country, where the mangy, roving, hungry, four-legged desperadoes seemed to be a good image of the land, described as 'a living, breathing picture of want'.

About 800 km (500 miles) north-west of Independence, after many weary days, the land began to hump and break up, whipped by strong dry winds into fantastic shapes of tortured rock. The trail followed the Platte and then the North Platte rivers, past the modest square wooden stockade of Fort Laramie, then it left the south-bending river and headed through a moonscape of twisted stone to the Sweetwater River and South Pass at the southern end of the Wind River Range (Wyoming). At the Sweetwater was Independence Rock, the best-known landmark on the Oregon Trail, where travellers carved their names into the grey dome-shaped mound. Jim Bridger's name was there, though the famous mountain man could neither read nor write. Soon after, the Wind River Range loomed up away to the right, towering cold and

ice-blue to more than 4000 m (13,000 ft). Below the tree-line were heavily timbered slopes, while at their root was South Pass, less of a narrow cleft than a wide valley of sagebrush, where the grade was so easy that only the parting of the streams, those of the Sweetwater going east and those of the Green (a major tributary of the mighty Colorado) going south-west, showed that this was, indeed, the continental divide.

At this point, the western pioneer entered truly into his promised land, gazing in alarm at a tempestuous and poverty-stricken world. Far to the south were the ragged peaks between which the Colorado river carved its way into Arizona. Immediately to the west was the main stream of the Green river, which flowed southwards to join the Colorado. Near the Green river's source in the Wind River Range rose the Snake river, which flows in a gigantic arc, south-west, west, and north, around the mountains of Idaho, to its rendezvous with the Columbia river in Washington state. The Oregon Trail lay through a vast, barren region between the Rockies and Coast ranges: the Columbia plateau to the north, a bleak scarred lava plain strangled by low, spiky vegetation; and the Great Basin of Nevada to the south, a desert of rattlesnakes and sand and sagebrush. 'A melancholy and strange looking country', John Charles Frémont called all this land, 'one of fracture, and violence, and fire'. With relief, the exhausted wanderer stumbled through the last mountain passes, seeking the rain-washed green of the Willamette valley beyond the Cascades in the north, or the sparkling southern airs of the lower California coast, where the Pacific swell growled at the foot of little cliffs.

A hard land made hard men. They set out meaning to endure, and they looked like it. The mountain traveller sat on his mule or unkempt pony, his weather-creased face framed with wild hair. He wore a shirt of flannel or skin, leather breeches with blanket leggings, and a buffalo robe. His feet were strapped in strips of blanket and shod in deerskin moccasins. A gun rested before him, and he tied a blanket-roll with extra moccasins behind the saddle. Saddle-bags on either side contained his meagre gear. At his belt he hung bullet pouch and powder horn, a tobacco sack, and flints for fire-making. A butcher's knife and an axe were fastened by leather thongs to the pommel.

A more gentlemanly traveller might set out with a little more elegance: perhaps a wide-brimmed felt hat, or a fringed and decorated leather shirt. He might have two pistols in holsters and a silver-trimmed Mexican saddle. But at the end of the trail gentlemen and ruffians were hard to tell apart. The Harvard scholar Francis Parkman started his western journey in style, but returned from the West in a 'red flannel shirt belted around the waist like a frock', and below that 'an extraordinary article, manufactured by a squaw out of smoked buckskin'.

OPPOSITE St Louis, seen here in George Catlin's painting of 1832, was a starting point for emigrants to the West. Most of them took a riverboat up the Missouri to the little town of Independence, where the Oregon Trail began. The paddle steamer *Yellowstone* plied between St Louis and the fur-trade centre of Fort Union, 2500 km (1550 miles) upstream at the junction of the Missouri and Yellowstone rivers.

Hazards of the Trail

The West was a great leveller. Survival demanded a democratic sharing. The weariness and dangers of the march allowed no special privileges. If a man was to get through, he must pull his weight. Summer heat and winter storms bore down on all alike. Horses stumbled in prairie-dog holes or tripped on dizzy mountain tracks. Dust clogged eyes, nose, and mouth. The white blindness of the snowstorm drove men and animals to the precipice edge, and sometimes over it. A thousand streams and rivers had to be forded or swum. Pack-horses and mules were coaxed out of quicksands, whipped into roaring waters, or hauled frantic and snorting up muddy banks. And at night, arriving parched or drenched at the evening camp, men lay down to the howl of marauding wolves and the vicious hum of numberless mosquitoes.

The evening camp was the only relaxation. The horses were hobbled, the blankets spread. On a fire of brushwood or buffalo dung, meat roasted on spits or boiled in the kettle. As the light failed, friendly stars hung in a limitless summer sky and the wind rustled the cottonwoods. A man sang a coarse ballad, rib-bones were chewed clean. The fire died to embers, a horse snuffled in the dark, then the vast night settled on the blanket-wrapped figures.

In the morning, the weariness began again, marching towards an end that was almost too distant to contemplate. Men travelled light, for each extra pound hurt. Coffee was the luxury most desired; sugar and hardtack were good, but not necessary. For the rest, one lived off the land. There were wild fruits, berries and roots in season. Anything small that ran, swam or flew was caught and eaten. In good times there was deer or elk. There were native dogs, which the Indians relished and the white man ate at a pinch. But most of all there was the American bison, known throughout the West as the buffalo.

The great, shaggy, lumbering beast 1.8 m (6 ft) at the shoulder and often weighing nearly 1000 kg (almost 1 ton), was the universal provider. Throughout the Great Plains and the foothills of the Rockies, ranging in herds that numbered millions, the buffalo gave everything that the western pioneer needed. From the carcass came huge amounts of meat; from the hide, a host of useful

By the time the migration westward was in full swing in the 1830s, women and children were hitting the trail along with the menfolk. The safest way to travel was in a wagon train with an experienced pathfinder at its head. When Albert Bierstadt painted this vivid scene of sunset on the prairie in 1871, half a century's hoof-marks and wheel ruts had made the main trails easy to follow.

commodities was made including trousers and tents, saddle-bags and boats. And after 1830, when over-trapping began to make the beaver scarce, buffalo became an important item of western trade, until careless greed virtually wiped out even this prolific giant.

The buffalo was a storehouse of plenty, and it also gave the West its favourite sport: the buffalo hunt. When the panicky herd began to move, thundering with the power and noise of an express locomotive, the blood quickened in every westerner. He tightened the girth, laid spurs to his horse, and was off. Guiding his mount with his knees, the hunter went roaring into the dust cloud, firing and reloading on the run, spitting a new bullet into his muzzle-loader then whamming it home with blows of the stock on the saddle. Galloping madly, drunk with the chase, and caring for nothing but buffalo, he charged on until bullets were spent or his foam-flecked horse pulled up lame or winded. 'I myself', wrote Francis Parkman after a hunt, 'felt as if drenched in warm water'.

Everything was used from the dead beast: the prime meat, the offal, the lights, the bones; raw liver was a delicacy, seasoned sometimes with a little gunpowder; yards of intestine, lightly roasted, were swallowed by the foot-length. For the great social occasion of the west, the meeting at the fur-company rendezvous, mighty quantities of buffalo meat were essential. A hungry mountain man could put away almost 3 kg (6½ pounds) at a sitting.

To the favourite rendezvous – Pierre's Hole or Jackson Hole, snuggling in the valley of the Snake – Indian and white man came, eager for the yearly 'relax'. Straight alcohol – still called whiskey – was unloaded from tin canisters. The trappers were paid off, and the trade goods laid out. For a few days the eccentric loners of the West revelled in rough company. It was a wild time. Most were drunk; fighting and gambling were other occupations. Indian girls were courted with ribbons and trinkets. Informal marriages were made and broken. Then once again to the drink. Calmly, at the end of the day, the new wives collected their broken heroes and laid them in the underbrush to recover.

All this was witnessed by the Indians who had come to trade, to drink, to gamble, and to be astonished by the white man. Sometimes the tribes

Map of the most important western trails.

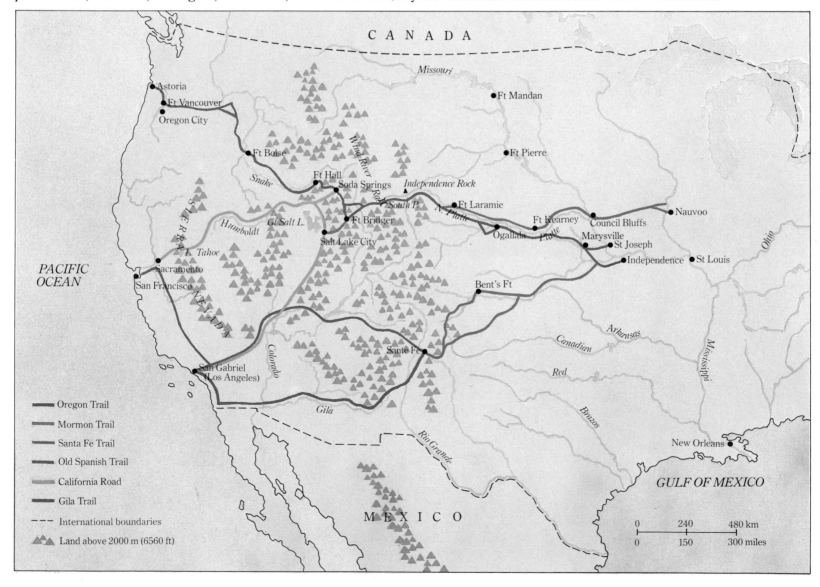

A mid-day halt on the Oregon trail. The emigrants shelter from the sun within the covered wagon, while their cattle, pigs and poultry rest or graze nearby. Bierstadt's sketch (1858) shows the wagon by the Platte, a wide but shallow and easily forded river whose course was followed by the Oregon Trail for hundreds of miles deep into the Rockies.

put on their own show, a rousing cavalry charge with war whoops and rifle volleys. Then they mingled into the swirl of bodies, taking a drink where they could, matching the white man in fantastic and uncouth behaviour. Gambling was their special passion. Swaying and chanting for luck, an Indian would bet all he had on a lightning hand palming a bit of polished bone in the native version of the three-card trick. At last, wretched from liquor and overeating, with money spent and goods lost, both whites and Indians limped back to the relentless hardship of their daily lives.

All this was a man's world. And for Americans the West remained strictly the province of men until the 1830s. It was unthinkable to allow a white woman into this wilderness. Even if she could withstand the dangers of the life, how, in all decency, was a woman in a long skirt to ride a mule through the Rockies? And as for wagons, could they complete the Oregon Trail? The track was thought to be too hazardous. Spokes shrank in the desert and broke in the mountains; the wheels fell off. Wagons got bogged down or stuck, or were too large for the path. Gradients were too steep, surfaces too pitted and rock-strewn. The experienced Rocky Mountain Company had tried wagons and failed. Besides, there were ferocious Indians, tribes 'whose very names are abominations'. Asked a scornful journalist in 1832: 'Did any white man ever cross the Rocky Mountains who will say that a white woman could have followed him?'

Women Cross the Continent

Against this evidence of the experts, it took a group of innocents to send the first women on the trail. In 1831 four Indians from the far north-west had arrived in St Louis to see the sights. No one knew if they were seeking religion, but a half-breed Christ-

The medical missionary Marcus Whitman was taking his newly-married wife Narcissa to the West, and they were accompanied by Henry and Eliza Spalding. These were to be the first American women to cross the continent.

The party set out with two farm wagons, one light and one heavy. They had 14 horses, 6 mules, 4 milch cows, and 13 steers. A couple of lads (one a Nez Percé) drove the animals, and a white 'mechanic' looked after the group. The signs were bad. Before they reached St Louis, old western hands warned them that the women would be destroyed. And if natural dangers spared them, then the 'unrestrained passion' of primitive tribes would undo them. But the women refused to be dismayed. Narcissa – for whom the journey was a honeymoon – was young, serene, and competent. And Eliza, though not in good health, was lively and shrewd.

In May 1836 they left St Louis, hurrying after the fur caravan which would take them at least as far as the trappers' rendezvous on the Green river, beyond South Pass. Overtaking the fur brigade on the Platte, and settling into its tail-plume of dust, the missionary ladies very soon knew the full misery of western travel. In June it rained, the air was poisonous with mosquitoes; the party was without a tent. The big cart bogged. A thousand streams were in seasonal flood. To unload and ferry goods by bullboat 20 times a day exhausted their muscles and patience. Native dogs ate the buffalo-skin covering of the bullboat. The little herd of animals was slow and awkward, backing and lowing and bolting at the river crossings, and invariably last into evening camp. The ladies, conspicuous in calico, plodded always in the dirt, mud or dust of the fur column. And at the midday 'nooning' rest, or when the creaking missionary wagons swung last into place in the hollow square of the evening encampment, inquisitive, prying faces of furmen and Indians popped round every corner, giving the women no privacy.

Immediately upon arrival at rest-place or camp there was the meal to get ready. They had stores on the wagons, and the luxury of milk and cream from the cows. But stores had to be used sparingly, and the usual diet was buffalo meat three times a day. 'I relish it well, and it agrees with me', Narcissa wrote. By the end of July, however, she was not so sure and sighed for pork and potatoes. The women had to learn frontier skills: to make a fire with dung, to bake bread in an iron skillet. They served the food in tin plates on the ground and ate with hunting knives; but they tried hard to keep a few civilized graces, spreading a cloth and using forks carved from sticks. After a hasty toilet, with dresses brushed clean of prairie dirt and with hair tied up, the ladies were escorted to the meal. Delicate Eliza became sick, but Narcissa 'was never so content and happy before'. By the time the party reached the rendezvous she was pregnant.

ian Wyandot convinced himself that these heathens needed help and wrote stirring letters to missionary societies in the east. Within two years the Christians were awake and anxious to bring salvation to 'these wandering sons of our native forests'. In 1834 Jason Lee set out for the Columbia river with a Methodist mission. This upright moralist had an adventurous year. Perhaps he wondered who were the more degenerate: white men who gulped blood from the pulsating heart of a newly-killed buffalo, or Indians who ate lice gathered from each other's hair. After reaching the Columbia, Lee decided that the Flatheads of his mission field were beyond his grasp; he retired to the lush green valleys of the Willamette.

Two years later, after much trouble with the Board for Foreign Missions, another religious group followed Lee. This was an extraordinary party, for it included not just one but two women.

There was much sickness that year in the West. Dysentery and diarrhoea were common. A cholera epidemic convulsed sufferers with cramps and shivering. Whitman, a doctor, had few remedies apart from bleeding or a good purge with salt and water. He did what he could, and made many a forlorn tramp to comfort those whose pains were really beyond his skill. But the presence of a doctor was an encouragement, and even Jim Bridger thought it worthwhile to have an old, embedded arrowhead dug out of his tough hide.

In July the missionaries reached the rendezvous on the Green river. The two women were greeted by a line of Nez Percé squaws who gave them ceremonious but hearty kisses, a custom they had learnt from white trappers. Then the massed horsemen of the Bannocks, Shoshones, Flatheads, and Nez Percés, in full regalia, swept by in a tempestuous charge. Naturally, the white women were something of a sensation, and there was much poking and open-mouthed staring. The mountain men were fascinated, too, and took every opportunity to button-hole these strange creatures from an almost forgotten past. Narcissa had the chance to press on her amazed audience two mule-loads of religious tracts. In the midst of tiresome attentions, both ladies kept their good humour.

So far the journey was reckoned a success. Whitman, speaking for most of the party, wrote cheerfully to the Mission Board. Only Spalding added a sour note: 'Never send another mission over these mountains', he wrote, 'if you value life and money'. His gloomy warning soon seemed justified. Led now by a Hudson's Bay Company brigade, the missionaries struggled towards the Columbia, still with the heavy wagon that Whitman refused to abandon. Progress with this wagon was a nightmare. It turned over; it broke its axles; it bogged down and stuck; and it nearly drowned its mules. 'Have six weeks' journey before us', Narcissa noted. 'Will the Lord give me patience to endure it?' The high summer heat was searing. They had to push on, no longer able to afford the 'nooning' rest. The cattle were foot-sore, gaunt-ribbed, and 'mad for the mosquitoes'. The sagebrush of the Columbia Plateau was 'so stiff and hard' that wagon and animals could hardly advance. Narcissa suffered the sickness of early pregnancy. The heat, the weariness and the diet dragged her down. 'I can scarce eat it', she wrote of the dried buffalo meat, 'it appears so filthy, but it will keep us alive'. Alive, yes – but only just. Wretched beyond belief, they crossed the Blue Mountains of north-east Oregon and hurried with rising joy into the Columbia valley. In the early morning of 1 September 1836 they reached Fort Walla Walla. Narcissa wept.

The efforts of missionaries had shown that the western crossing could be made – although with great difficulty – by women, by wagons, and by cattle. A way was open for emigrants, for families going west with goods and chattels and herds. Seasoned mountain men were available as guides. Points of rest and security along the way had been provided by the construction, in 1834, of Fort Laramie, Fort Hall, and Fort Boise – scruffy little outposts behind simple wooden stockades, but still havens in the wilderness. And when the success of the missionaries was learned in the East, emigrant societies bloomed. From 1840 onwards the ordinary American man and woman jostled to find a place in the western sun.

This was a migration of tenderfoots. They gathered at Independence, on the Missouri, a disorganized rabble more fit for crossing New York's Broadway than the prairie. 'Whoo, ha! Go it, boys!' the Independence *Expositor* cheered, watching frantic efforts to get man and beast in order. 'We're in a perfect *Oregon fever*'. Somehow the columns got away, stringing out sullenly onto the prairie. Francis Parkman came across them at Fort Laramie in 1846. 'Tall awkward men, in brown homespun; women with cadaverous faces and long lank figures', he wrote. 'They seemed like men totally

out of their element, bewildered and amazed, like a troop of schoolboys lost in the woods'. They amazed the Indians too. 'They could scarcely believe that the earth contained such a multitude of white men'. Parkman correctly foresaw that this slow, relentless invasion was dangerous for the future. Indian wonder was giving way to indignation; 'and the result, unless vigilantly guarded against, may be lamentable in the extreme'. Forty years later, with the Indians cowed and beaten and huddled into desolate reservations, Parkman was proved right. These dull, relentless plodders, dragging themselves wearily towards the horizon, inherited the land.

In time, a rough routine developed on the trail. 'It is on the stroke of seven', wrote Jesse Applegate, who commanded a cow column in 1834; 'there's rushing to and fro, the cracking of the whips, the loud command to oxen, and what seems to be inextricable confusion'. But the trumpet sounds from the front, and once again the bellowing, awkward mob gets in motion, perhaps a hundred wagons and several thousand head of cattle.

The track was well-beaten as far as Fort Hall on the Snake river. Then the California settlers peeled off south-west into the desert, into the notorious Humboldt valley and the Nevada desert, while the Oregon folk followed the Snake down to the Columbia and on to the Pacific coast.

The Mormon Migration

An established method and route, which could be followed with a fair degree of safety, was a great encouragement to others. When the Mormons decided to flee from trouble and persecution in Illinois, they had no hesitation about heading west. When they left Nauvoo, on a snow-bound 1 March 1846, their exact destination was a mystery, but they were soundly prepared for the journey. Each family group was advised of its needs: 1 wagon, 3 yokes of oxen, 5 cows, 3 sheep; 450 kg (1000 lb) of flour and 9 kg (20 lb) of sugar; a tent, clothes, bedding, tools, implements, and seeds. All this was estimated to cost about 250 dollars. In a year and a quarter of slow migration, stirred on by a brass band and guided for part of the journey by Jim Bridger, some

An emigrant family poses beside a wagon containing their worldly possessions. The wagons, drawn by horses or oxen, were popularly known as prairie schooners because their white canvas tops looked like sails when seen from a distance across the vast western plains.

12,000 Mormons with 3000 wagons struggled through all the usual and appalling hazards of the march to their final place of settlement in the Utah desert. On 19 July 1847 they saw for the first time the Great Salt Lake on its bleak, burning plain: 'instinctively, as if by inspiration', wrote one of their number, 'we raised our hats from our heads, and then shouted, "Hosannah to God and the Lamb!"'

The Mormons were not alone in giving thanks for divine guidance. There was a religious fervour about the westward movement. These wandering folk were believers not only in the hand of the Lord but also in the certainty of their destiny to possess and shape the new land. It needed an inspiration such as this to turn greenhorns into pioneer heroes; to turn corn-chandlers, carters, and small-time hatters into landbreakers capable of conquering what has been called 'the lawless interval between the abodes of civilized man'. It was not easy for women to see their children playing in 'quagmires of black dirt', or to find their little house on wheels surrounded by 'yellow pools, steaming up vapours redolent of the savour of death'. In a pathetic space, under a dark spread of sour-smelling canvas, they tried to achieve the order and comfort of a home. They saw their children wasting with dysentery. Their men reeled from mountain sickness and suffered the 'black canker' of scorbutic fever. Babies were delivered on the frozen ground of a filthy tent, with the temperature outside at 20° below. During the winter of their migration, the Mormons buried more than 600 people.

Despite the hardships the emigrants battled through. They conquered the trail, and they made prairie and mountain productive. And naive, vulnerable newcomers followed in their thousands, rattling over the ruts of the now-well-worn ground, crossing 3200 km (2000 miles) in the wake of a plodding ox-train. These were people who had 'no previous preparation, relying only on the fertility of

Fort Laramie, on the North Platte river near Wyoming's eastern border, was an important trading centre for white and Indian fur trappers from the early years of the 19th century. Later it also became a key staging post on the Oregon Trail – for long the last permanent white settlement before the passage over the Rockies.

ABOVE Salt Lake City (Utah) in 1853, some six years after the Mormons arrived at the barren site their leader Brigham Young claimed to have seen in a vision. The emigrants had been driven out of their Illinois community of Nauvoo, on the Mississippi.

OPPOSITE James Marshall poses in front of Sutter's Mill, near Sacramento, where he discovered the first gold to be found in California in 1848. This historic photograph was taken the following year.

their invention'. Yet, whatever peril and hardship either nature or the Indians could throw at them, Jesse Applegate wrote proudly, 'they are always found ready and equal to the occasion, and always conquerors. May we not call them men of destiny?'

The Western Ideal

They were looking for an ideal, for peace and security such as Mark Twain thought he had found by the edge of Lake Tahoe, in Nevada, when he tried to take possession of a little tract of timbered land. 'We did not see a human being,' he wrote, 'or hear any sounds but those that were made by the wind and the waves, the sighing of the pines, and now and then the far off thunder of an avalanche. The forest about us was dense and cool, and the sky above us was cloudless and brilliant with sunshine.'

The ideal was hard to find, but the pioneer struggled towards it. At the end of the trail, when the prospect tempted him, or when weariness brought him to a halt, the pioneer immigrant settled on a small portion of the 'range' and marked it off. He built a log-cabin, chinked with mud and moss. He cleared and fenced a field of a few acres. He planted corn and a 'truck patch' of cabbages, potatoes, beans and squash. He possessed, maybe, a cow, a horse, a couple of hogs. If he were lucky, he had good timber and water. He 'pays no rent, and feels

as independent as the lord of the manor'. He began to overcome the wilderness, and other immigrants, attracted by his tiny kingdom of established order, stopped there also and dropped roots in the same part of the territory.

And then, perhaps, the true pioneer began to feel cramped by an incoming population. There was another farm a mile down the road; a well-beaten track led to a simple settlement; someone had built a bridge over a troublesome creek. The true pioneer lacked elbow room. He sold cabin and field to a newcomer and once again 'broke for the high timber.' But in the place that he left there was the beginnings of a community. A short row of wooden frame houses sprang up, bordering a dusty Main Street. A raised board-walk kept feet out of summer dirt and winter mud. Some slightly grander buildings sat around a 'plaza' – 'an unfenced, level vacancy, with a liberty pole in it, and very useful for public auctions, horse trades, and mass meetings.' A council of worthies began to conduct business from clapboard bedrooms. In a short time, a Court House bloomed amid the huddle of shanties. Rough fellows in bear-skin caps, mackinaw blankets and leggings, carrying Old Bess rifles and hunting knives, gazed in wonder at this evidence of young civilization. 'Yes, sir,' they assured each other heartily, 'we are an Almighty people.'

Bonanza

*Nothing increased the pace of westward migration
so dramatically as the discovery of gold
in 1848. All over the eastern states workmen
downed tools, clerks abandoned safe jobs,
soldiers deserted—all to join the mad
rush to California....*

On 24 January 1848 a labourer, James Marshall, building a sawmill on the American river just above Sacramento (California), noticed some yellow grits in the tailrace of the mill. He took the bright particles to his boss, John Sutter. Then the two men locked the door, got out an encyclopedia for instruction, and put the fragments of mineral to various tests. After a while they straightened up and sighed deeply. They had discovered gold.

Sutter swore his men to secrecy. He was a Swiss emigrant who had taken advantage of the American victory over Mexico to carve a little princedom out of Californian land, and he knew that gold fever would destroy the peace and security of his New Helvetia. And he was right. The news could not be kept bottled up and soon had spread to San Francisco and Monterey, two sleepy settlements that had dozed through many years of Spanish and Mexican occupation. Now Yankee energy kicked them awake. 'Our town was startled out of its quiet dreams today,' wrote Walter Colton, Monterey's mayor. In May, samples of the gold arrived, and the town emptied. Workmen dropped their tools, soldiers threw down their rifles and deserted. A boarding-house keeper abandoned her guests and dashed off without collecting the money due to her. 'All were off for the mines,' wrote Colton, 'some on horses, some on carts, some on crutches, and one went in a litter.'

The French consul reported that the same thing happened in San Francisco. The town was just starting to expand, under new American rule, when suddenly two-thirds of the population disappeared into the hills. The commander of the Pacific Naval Squadron complained that not only riff-raff were deserting, but also petty officers of long and honourable service. In California neither 'hope of reward or fear of punishment' could prevent this mad exodus.

By the end of the year samples of Californian gold had reached the east coast, and the mint in Philadelphia pronounced them to be good. The migration westward, already in strong flow towards the free land, suddenly swelled to a torrent of the hopeful with an incurable ache for quick riches. 'Everybody,' the Washington *Intelligencer* reported in January 1849, 'now talks of gold, dreams of it, or digs for it.' The race of the Forty-niners to the dream-mountain of gold had begun.

The stores of the great cities competed with each other to sell 'California Goods': six-barrel revolvers, Allen's Selfcocking Pistol, Bowie knives, wax-taper matches, hatchets, money belts made 'exclusively for gold'. Whispers were flying everywhere of the extraordinary wealth just waiting to be picked up. A man fresh from California had seen a 3 kg (7 lb) lump of gold. Another man had panned 16 kg (36 lb) in one day; yet another had made 12,000 dollars in a week. Everyone in the east with a taste for adventure bought a gun, a knife, some camping gear and a California guide, and hit the trail as fast as possible. When a gentlemanly company of Washington speculators reached the Missouri ferry-crossing at St Joseph (north of Kansas City) in April 1849, they found the ferry was fully booked until July.

Soon the trail got hard and the fortune hunters became the victims of their own haste and foolishness. They struggled into the mountains with feather beds, quilts and comforters, pots and pans, knives and forks, and good bone china. 'Many of these things,' wrote one witness, 'are about as much use to the emigrant as two tails to a dog. Talk about clothing! Some had trunks full of white shirts and plug hats.' Gradually the dross was thrown out and littered the track. Cumbersome wagons were chopped up to make pack-saddles or burnt. Trunks, ploughs, anvils, grindstones, ovens, stoves, kegs, food, clothing and domestic articles without number lay on all sides. 'All the debris of 19th-century man began to clutter the Garden of the West.' Starvation and disease took a heavy toll. The crude crosses on wayside graves were the best milestones to the goldfields. The loss of man and animals was most severe in the grim desert of the Humboldt valley, between the Rockies and the Sierra Nevada. Without grazing, and poisoned by alkaline water, animals lay down and did not get up. The hot wind picked the bones clean.

The lonely land of the Sierra Nevada, once the haunt of a few mountain men, was suddenly overrun by an anxious, irritable host of fortune seekers, living on rumour and wild exaggeration, hustling from one hopeful site to another. 'There is gold here in abundance,' a prospector wrote in 1850, 'but it requires patience and hard labour, with some skill and experience to obtain it.' Placer gold, at first widely available in the gravel beds and sandbanks of crushed in a stamp-mill and the gold separated out with mercury. Stocked with 'a good store of pork and beans' the Forty-niner camped nearby, and in a short time he could 'expect to lay up money'.

In the shifting world of rootless adventurers, who could tell how many fortunes were made? Wave after wave they came on, as frantic as wasps around a honey pot. The early techniques were primitive and wasteful, but a few found riches and lost them, fewer made fortunes and kept them, and most disappeared into obscurity and ruin. The gold was certainly

Within a year of the sensational discovery at Sutter's Mill the goldrush had begun. E. Hall Martin's *Mountain Jack and the Wandering Miner*, painted in 1850, shows a would-be prospector seeking the advice of a trapper in the Sierra Nevada.

there in large amounts. The California Bureau of Mines valued the 1849 output at 10 million dollars; by 1852 it had risen to 81 million. Gold was the chief attraction, but not the only one. Travellers on their way to California had found likely looking minerals in the Washoe Mountains of the new Nevada Territory, but had hurried on to the true gold of California. Towards the end of the 1850s, as the early gold fever was abating, some prospectors decided to take another look at the 'blue stuff' that

streams, was soon worked out. Then the gold-bearing rock lying in outcrops and near the surface was attacked with simple tools. With a pick, a shovel, a strong knife, a horn spoon, and a cradle, the gold hunter was ready for business. Diggings from the riverbed were sluiced into the cradle, then shaken and sieved. With luck, the gold particles remained behind. In the dry diggings the rock was

Prospectors set off for the California goldfields. By the end of 1850 many new towns had sprung up in the neighbourhood of the mines; and when the seams had been picked clean a year or two later, they were just as quickly abandoned.

had been dug out of Mount Davidson. It was found to be a rich silver ore.

This was the beginning of the famous Comstock Lode. Virginia City (Nevada), a few miles southeast of Reno, sprang up around the mine, and within two years had a population of more than 10,000. In the 30 years after 1860 the Comstock produced silver valued at 340 million dollars. Many rich seams were tapped beneath the mountain, but the finest of all was the 'Big Bonanza', a vein discovered more than 300 m (1000 ft) down in 1873, and so big that it was said 'a blind man driving a four-horse team could have followed it in a snow storm'.

The Rocky Mountains, too, were a storehouse of valuable minerals from end to end. Hardly a year went by without some new strike being whispered down the grapevine. Then men fell over each other to struggle into the wilderness, and within a few months a shanty town of miners would be standing in wastes of mud and refuse. Colorado was studded with mines that flared and died in a few brief years, most of them dependent on the new city of Denver for supplies and finance. A lucky find on the edge of the Arizona desert, near the Mexican border, brought the sweating riff-raff to Tombstone. The Mormons in Utah capitalized on the good fortune of silver mines in the mountains around Salt Lake City. Gold, silver, and lead were found in the north, in Idaho. Butte (Montana), near the headwaters of the Missouri, was first a magnet for gold prospectors, then a silver mining camp, and finally one of the largest of the western copper mines. There was copper also in Utah – in Bingham, 'a sewer five miles long' – and gold in the Black Hills of Dakota. Indian treaties had been re-drawn before, as soon as valuable minerals were found on their lands. This happened in Dakota, in 1874-5, provoking a Sioux uprising. But the white man was not to be denied 'his' treasure. The Indians were brutally suppressed and Deadwood (how well it was named!) rose on their bones. In the half century after the first California gold-rush of 1849, the whole American expanse of the Rockies, from the Gulf of California to the Columbia river, was probed and picked over by five generations of fortune hunters.

Grubbing for Gold

The early Forty-niners, setting out with such energy and such high hopes, made their search appear something of a carnival. Americans, Mexicans, Indians, emigrants from all over Europe, they brought to the goldfields a dozen languages and a thousand strange habits. When the traveller Bayard Taylor visited the California diggings on the Mokelumne river in 1849 he found a colourful and busy community. The camp nestled in the river bottom, with the majestic white peaks of the Sierra Nevada high above. A scattering of white tents surrounded the diggings. A little distance away the Mexican miners had put up in three weeks a village of sapling huts, without walls and roofed with loose boughs. There was a 'hotel' run by a wily French mountain man, but this was nothing more than an airy shelter with plank tables for food and for gambling, and a plentiful supply of liquor.

The diggings themselves were in a small area of rough, rocky land where a dry ravine met the shrunken riverbed. The whole place was burrowed with laborious workings, hacked out with simple tools under a hot sun. The work was hard and boring, yet a constant trickle of golden grains kept the men lively. When Taylor saw men stooped knee-deep in water, grubbing for hours in dirt and gravel, he thought gold fever was easy to resist; 'but when the shining particles were poured out lavishly from a tin basin, I confess there was a sudden itching in my fingers to seize the heaviest crowbar and the biggest shovel.' The morning's work produced about 2.7 kg (6 lb) of gold; in general, a man who worked with patience and tenacity might expect to get from 50 to 100 g (2 to 4 oz) a day.

But many had no inclination for the hard slog of the diggings, and preferred to ride their luck. Taylor met a doctor who, resting from the noon heat, idly picked at the ground and turned up a 1 kg (2.2 lb) lump of gold. Many Americans hired Mexicans or Indians to do their digging. Other prospectors, of all races, would rather go over abandoned holes than dig new ones themselves. 'They compared the diggings,' wrote Taylor, 'to a lottery, in which people grew rich only by accident or luck.' The conventional ties between hard work, satisfaction, and rewards did not hold in the goldfields. A few casual thrusts might unearth a fortune, yet a year of hard digging could end with nothing. No wonder, then, that prospectors were not prudent. It was not unusual to see dirty ruffians in broken boots 'drinking their champagne at $10 a bottle, or warming in the smoky camp-kettle their tin canisters of turtle-soup and lobster-salad.'

Taylor met an eccentric called Buckshot who lived alone in a small tent, worked most days, and had dug out, in a year or so, perhaps 40,000 dollars worth of gold. He spent every penny on luxurious eating, choosing oysters and hams and dried fruits and special vegetables and Chinese delicacies, all washed down daily with a bottle of champagne. Then full of good things, and broke, he took his pickaxe back to the diggings.

Gambling was another common indulgence, which was not surprising since prospecting was in itself the great gamble. At Mokelumne, Taylor noted at least a dozen 'monte' tables, well-used especially by Mexicans. Where the ordinary values of money and exchange were topsy-turvy, it hardly mattered if a man lost a month's gold in a night. There was plenty more in the hills. Miners did many things to excess; and where gold and gambling are there to corrupt, and drink to heat up the passions,

Panning for gold in California in 1849. The miner has loaded his pan with deposits from the bed of the stream. Now he agitates the pan, hoping to see a few golden particles separate out from the mud and gravel.

and easy, but few cared to risk it. The punishment was too painful.

Boom Towns

The fortune hunters of the early days, searching for placer gold, formed a restless mass of individualists, carrying their primitive technology on their backs, anxious to 'git and git out'. Their dwellings were temporary and they had no settled communities. But when, at a later stage, minerals had to be properly mined and dug out from deep veins, boom towns sprung up almost overnight. Virginia City, the Nevada town of the Comstock silver miners, grew amazingly. In 1860 it was a few shanties on a bare mountain slope, less than 20 years later it had a church of cathedral-like size, an opera house, more than 100 saloons, and a hotel with the only elevator west of Chicago.

No other mining town reached the grandeur of Virginia City, and most fell very far short. The pattern of development was a familiar one: first a rash of grubby tents around the strike; then a single street of jerrybuilt wooden huts hastily thrown together behind false-fronts, and giving on to an unmade road which was a dust patch in summer and a mud bath in winter; and finally a small town of some civic buildings in stone and many weather-beaten wooden houses where the citizens made valiant efforts to lead lives of reasonable comfort and dignity.

Some towns never reached that last stage. Many, like Last Chance Gulch and Deadwood, barely progressed beyond a single street lined with bars and gambling halls sitting on a mound of mine-tailings and domestic refuse. A mining expert, Ross Browne, who visited Virginia City in its earliest days, saw 'tents of canvas, of blankets, of brush, of potato sacks, and old shirts, with empty whiskey barrels for chimneys; smoky hovels of mud and stone; coyote holes in the mountain-side forcibly seized and held by men.' Everything was covered with mud and rubbish, as if the dregs and leavings of society had fallen from a cloudburst. Towns like this were raw places for men, but for women they were abominable. An early pamphlet for women lamented the absence of churches, of theatres, of shops, of parties, of balls, of gossip, of fashion, of newspapers, of books, of daily mail: 'no promenades, no rides, no drives; no vegetables but potatoes and onions, no milk, no eggs, no *nothing*.'

In these brash towns, good order was something of a problem. The miner in deep workings, unlike the prospector, was not an adventurer chancing his luck, but a wage-slave working in grim conditions. Ross Browne saw these miners as 'roaring, raving drunkards' living in towns filled with 'desperadoes of the vilest sort'. There was, in these places, a constant undercurrent of crime and violence, with a host of rogues and panders battening on to the wide-open town.

crime is likely to follow. 'The mines,' wrote one cynical observer who returned disappointed to Monterey, 'are loaded to the muzzle with vagabonds from every quarter of the globe, scoundrels from nowhere, rascals, pickpockets, thieves, gamblers, and assassins manufactured in hell for the express purpose of converting highways and byways into theatres of blood.'

The more temperate Bayard Taylor thought that the Mokelumne diggings had 'as much order and security as could be attained without a civil organization'. The miners governed themselves and a harsh justice was served out democratically. Taylor met a man sentenced to 100 lashes, a shaved head, and cropped ears for stealing 44 kg (97 lb) of gold. Men were kept in check by a fair but brutal severity. In a community without walls, theft was tempting

But very soon, as in the gold diggings, miners showed the strength of frontier democracy and managed to organize themselves long before the arrival of the apparatus of government from the east. Vigilantes caught and hanged the worst criminals with little trial and less fuss. Committees of civic-minded people founded schools, churches, theatres, libraries, newspapers; poetry readings and concerts were by no means rare, as well as prize-fights and vaudeville. Municipal offices were set in order, and ambitious frontiersmen, well pleased with themselves, itched to go east and put Washington to rights. 'Congregate a hundred Americans,' it was said, 'and they immediately lay out a city, form a State constitution and apply for admission to the Union, while twenty-five of them become candidates for the US Senate.'

The Goldrush Legacy

The frantic development of mining in the Rockies and the Sierra Nevada destroyed, as John Sutter had feared in 1848, the sleepy peace of the West. For generations southern California had jogged along, a thinly populated land of cattle and ranches. The first years of American migration had scarcely disturbed the land. Fur traders, mountain men and farming settlers work slowly, relying on time and the seasons for the gradual accumulation of their rewards. The first Americans in California, having won the land from Mexico, 'destroyed little that was

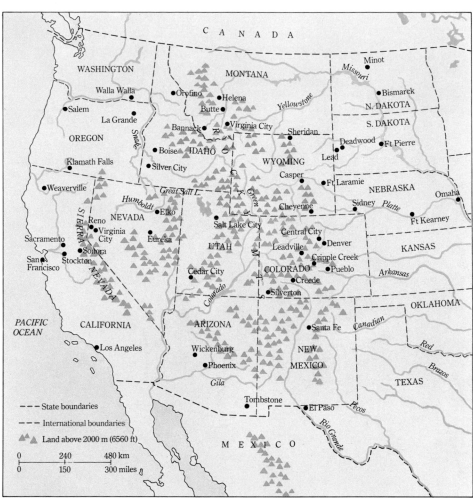

ABOVE Map of the main gold and silver mining locations in the mid-19th century.

LEFT The small Spanish settlement of San Francisco became the main port, supply centre, and clearing house for the California goldrush. By 1850, when this photograph of its dock area was taken, it had a population of 40,000.

old, created little that was new'. Then came gold fever and the arrival of the Forty-niners. In the blink of an eye Sutter's idyllic settlement at the junction of the Sacramento and American rivers was turned into the roaring gold town of Sacramento. The new town of Stockton, 60 km (40 miles) to the south, which had been a solitary Spanish ranch in the middle of a marsh, became in only four months 'a canvas town of 1000 inhabitants, and a port, with 25 vessels at anchor'. Bayard Taylor wrote that a firm had done 100,000 dollars worth of business in those four months. A building lot on the main street was selling for 6000 dollars and a single-storey clapboard house cost 15,000 dollars to build. A year

later, in 1850, a US Senator wondered at the rocketing ascent of California: in 1846 it had been a Mexican province 'unknown even to our usually immoderate desires'; in 1848-9 a 'mere military dependency' of the United States; but in 1850 it was 'a State, more populous than the least and richer than several of the greatest of our thirty States'.

The discovery of minerals was even more important in remote mountain territories than it was in California. The new territories of Idaho, Montana, Dakota, Utah, Nevada, Colorado, and Arizona would have found their difficult lands hard to develop had it not been for the finance, the trade, the technology, and most of all the population, which the mines brought in and encouraged. This was an extraordinary development – and it was bought at an extraordinary price in broken lives and ruined fortunes, in human waste and misery. 'Very many,' wrote a sorrowful prospector who saw it all happen, 'meet with bad success, and thousands will leave their bones here. Others will lose their health, contract diseases that they will carry to their graves.' An old Forty-niner, speaking after the terrible carnage of the Civil War, said that none of those fierce battles 'broke so many heartstrings and caused such widespread pain as did the California gold migration'.

Resources as well as lives were squandered and misplaced. The appetite of the mines for resources of all kinds starved the rest of the West. By 1850 the little Spanish settlement of San Francisco had grown into the main port and clearing-house for the gold-rush, with a population of some 40,000. The biggest settlement in the southern part of California was the cattle town of Los Angeles, with a population of only 1600. As the mines prospered, agriculture stagnated. Settlers, homesteaders and rural communities begged for capital to allow them to develop, yet mining speculation and finance had pushed interest rates to a dizzy height which modest communities could never afford. The consumption of the mines sucked the land dry. The deep galleries of the Comstock Lode swallowed 800 million board feet of timber supports, an appetite satisfied only by the plunder of public forest for miles around. Even the quarrels of the miners were wasteful. Claim and counter-claim were fought in the courts with energy and malice. Over a five-year period the Comstock spawned 245 lawsuits, an outpouring of time and money that enriched the lawyers and accounted for 10 per cent of the value of all the Comstock production.

The mining madness in California, Nevada Territory, and the Rocky Mountains is only one strange chapter in the whole strange history of the western migration. To some extent, *all* the emigrants were gamblers. They lived on hope and dreams, not certainties; and their actions were not always tied to logic and good sense. They flowed and ebbed as time and fortune took them, and expected suffering as well as success.

The discovery of valuable minerals, offering the daring a chance of instant riches, brought men running. Grim mountain towns, with no more comfort or dignity than a bed of nails, filled up as quickly as New Orleans at carnival. Then the bonanza passed. The worked-out mines were closed, and the dangerous, rowdy places became as quiet as the grave. The townsfolk drifted off to other business in another part of the West. They settled and multiplied, and gave the western states a raw energy and optimism that they had inherited from a generation of gold-hunters.

Cowboys, Cattle and Farmers

After the acquisition of Texas in 1848 the United
States found itself with an abundance of cattle
in the south and a ready market for beef in
the north-east. By 1870 the great
cattle drives to the Kansas railheads
were in full swing....

A quest for land took the emigrants to the West. From forests and fields and good soil in the east, they crossed the Missouri into a land more stark than welcoming: a vast, dry plain, a tangled upheaval of mountains, and finally a narrow coastal strip. Somewhere in this varied geography were the deep valleys, the pastures, the fertile earth, and the green woods that the pioneers sought. But they were hard to find, and for much of the trek westwards the land-hungry settler saw instead, stretching on every side, the huge dry expanse of the prairie. Here a thin soil supported little but grass; sparse stands of willow and cottonwood grew in the river bottoms, but the plain, for mile upon mile, was bare. The climate went to harsh extremes, from deep winter snows to a blistering summer heat. The land seemed too dry, despite the snow and the violence of the thunderstorms: large rivers shrivelled to pencils of brackish water creeping over wastes of gravel. There was plenty of land for the taking. But the homesteader in a new country needs water and timber in equal amounts, and these were very hard to come by. Almost the only encouragement to man in all this wilderness were the thriving herds of animals.

The horses and cattle were there long before the United States. Both had arrived with the Spaniards in the 16th century, and the descendants of those early animals were the nervous mustangs and the agile, wiry longhorns of the south-west. For 300 years Mexican *vaqueros* (cowhands) had tamed them, bred them, and ranched them. The hardy longhorns, acclimatized to the dry grasslands, were a large part of the prosperity of northern Mexico. This was the territory that became American in 1848 when the United States, after the Mexican War, took 1,300,000 km² (500,000 sq miles) of formerly Spanish land, including Texas and southern California. Suddenly the enlarged American nation found that it had an abundance of cattle. In the state of Texas it was said that there were six head of cattle for every person.

It was a problem to know what to do with all these animals. The Texans ate their fill of beef, sent some hides and tallow to the industrial north, and then left the carcasses to the scavengers. The longhorn was hard to drive, being a wayward beast with an intimidating spread of sharp horns. Unless prices were high, there was little incentive to trail them to the markets of the populous north-east.

Conditions improved for the cattle trade from about 1850. The hungry Forty-niners, flooding to the mines of the Rockies, created a small but good beef market in California. The profits were worthwhile despite the long drive through desert and Apache country; but a much larger market, swollen by rising population and the rapid growth of industry, awaited in the north and east. Beef prices climbed quickly. The problem in Texas, said one commentator, 'was to link a four-dollar steer to a forty-dollar market!'

In 1852 the northerner Tom Ponting left Illinois, money-belt stuffed with gold, determined to find the answer to this problem. His grand ambition was to drive a herd from Texas to New York. Going down to the cattle country, Ponting left the gold under the mattress of a trustworthy landlady until he had gathered about 700 steers. Then he and his partner set out on a two-year trail which took them, after 2400 km (1500 miles) by foot and 960 km (600 miles) by rail, to the New York Hundred Street Market in July 1854. The best animals fetched 80 dollars each. They were good-quality beef, the *Tribune* reported, though the long-legged beasts had 'something of a wild look'.

If the price was right, then, the hazardous business of trail-driving was worth it. But hardly had the trade begun when it seemed likely to fail. The Civil War of 1861-5 disrupted all commerce between North and South. Longhorns were carriers of a disease called splenic (or 'Texas') fever, to which they themselves were immune, but which they passed on to northern cattle breeds. By 1866 state quarantine laws had closed the trail to Texas cattle at the Kansas-Missouri line. Yet, at this very mo-

Arizona cowboy, from a painting by Frederic Remington. His gear includes a lariat for roping cattle and horses, leather chaps to protect his legs, a Colt six-shooter to drive off rustlers (white or Indian), and a neckerchief that could serve as a mask against the clouds of dust kicked up by the herd on the move.

ment, the North was clamouring for beef. On Christmas Day 1865 the 140 hectares (345 acres) of the Union Stock Yards were opened in Chicago. The meat-packing houses of Armour and Swift wanted all the cattle they could get.

The rescue of the southern trade, as the livestock dealer Joseph McCoy quickly realised, lay with the railways. If a depot could be established on the prairie to the north of Texas, then cattle could be trailed to the railhead, put on trucks and sent north fast and safely. In 1867, after a troublesome search, McCoy found a sleepy village near the end of the Kansas Pacific Railroad line. This was Abilene, 'a very small, dead place', a dozen log huts with dirt roofs and a saloon in a dark cabin. But it was ideal for McCoy. It was outside the hostile farming belt, it had water and grass, and it had some protection against Indians from nearby Fort Riley. In July McCoy struck a deal with the railroad. Within 60 days he had built a stockyard, a barn, an office, and a hotel. By late August the first herds were arriving. On 5 September 1867, 20 wagonloads left for Chicago. The age of cattle kingdoms and cowboys had arrived.

The Cattle Drive

Soon the northward trails were hoof-beaten highways filled yearly with a shifting mass of men and horses and thousands of cattle. Of several important trails, the Chisholm Trail from San Antonio to Abilene was the most famous. It was named after a half-breed Cherokee trader, but cunningly advertised and marked by McCoy. And McCoy's foresight and planning were well rewarded. In 1867 Abilene shipped out some 36,000 cattle; by 1870 the number had risen to 300,000.

'The longer he lived,' said an old cattleman of the longhorn, 'the meaner he became.' Everything in the management of this fast, aggressive brute called for courage, skill, and endurance in the cowboy. At the spring round-up the wild longhorns had to be forced or enticed out of their winter freedom. Some were roped by moonlight and left tied to quieten them; some were lured into corrals by tame cattle acting as decoys, or lulled out of dry gullies and underbrush by the soft singing of cowboys. And when the herd was gathered, animals unsuitable for the drive had to be cut out. To do this well was the highest art of the cowboy, man and horse in perfect

Map of the main cattle trails.

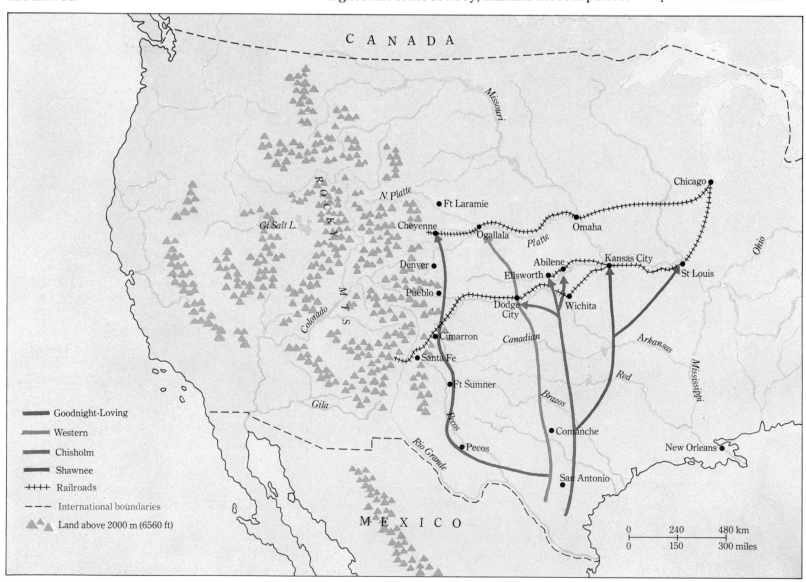

Charles M. Russell's *Bronco in a Riding Camp* shows an important prelude to the cattle drive: the breaking in of wild horses to be used on the trail. In the background stands the all-important chuck-wagon, the camp's mobile store-room and kitchen. The cook dispensed coffee and food from the wagon's tailgate.

co-ordination amid the thrashing hooves, while the man handled the lasso like a conjurer. Then came a spirited wrestling-match with each wild-eyed steer to force it onto its side so that its legs could be roped and it could be dragged to the branding-iron before hitting the trail.

Before sun-up on the day of departure the trail boss roused the cook; coffee was on the boil 'until it could float a pistol', and the cowboys saw to their horses. About 15 hands could control an average drive of some 2500 cattle, and each man would need up to 10 horses. A youth known as the wrangler took the spare horses and set off before the cattle. The cook, a wise old hand on whose skill and experience the good temper of the group depended, shook the chuck-wagon team into motion. The trail boss would ride ahead, scouting the route and choosing the night's camp site. The pointers at the front urged on the leading cattle. The other hands, in order of seniority, fanned out around the herd, with the drag riders behind to collect the weak and the lame – and to eat great mouthfuls of dust. The drive was away, heading for Abilene, six weeks of hard going to the north.

Longhorns were mean, cussed beasts, but

Texans swore that they were the best animals for trail-driving. They were very hardy and could keep going through drought and famine. They panicked less than other breeds, and if they did stampede they ran together so that they could be turned or 'milled' (kept circling) more easily. On the drive a veteran steer would take the lead, the rest falling into the same rough order day by day. It was considered that 32 km (20 miles) was a good day's march, the herd loafing and grazing through the morning, resting at noon, then hurrying along briskly as the cattle sniffed for a water-hole and the men looked forward to the cheerful clang of the frying-pan and the cook's 'Come and get it!'

The evening chuck (supper) was the great moment of the day, when the cook dumped onto tin plates plentiful amounts of an unvaried diet: beef, sourdough biscuits, beans, and bitter black coffee. Tired men sprawled around the fire, mending gear or playing a little poker for matches – they got no money until the end of the drive. In the dark, the nightwatch rode slowly out among the herd, crooning old cowboy favourites to still any restive cattle. In the camp, blankets were pulled up to the chin and large stetsons set to ward off the dew. Then, in the

dawn, the cook's brutal shout and more black coffee brought in another day.

Occasionally, in the night, a branch snapping or a dislodged stone sent the herd stampeding. This is what cattlemen feared most, for it was always dangerous and sometimes impossible to stop. The charging herd flattened everything in its path and generated enough heat, said Charles Goodnight (an early cattle king) 'almost to blister' men's faces. To go down before a stampeding herd was fatal. 'We found him among the prairie dog holes', wrote an old-timer of a fallen colleague. 'Horse and man were mashed into the ground as flat as a pancake. The only thing you could recognize was the handle of his six-shooter.' And if the stampede could not be turned or milled, the herd might destroy itself. On one drive, every animal plunged into a ravine near the Brazos river, Texas, which gave the place the melancholy name of Stampede Gulch.

Nor was the stampede the only danger. Storms could do as much damage. Col. Ike Pryor had a 500,000 dollar herd almost wiped out by a spring snow storm; another drive lost 78 horses, frozen to death overnight. Indians, especially Comanches and Kiowas, were often a problem: the 'friendly'

ones would run some of the animals off, and then bring them back for a reward; the hostile would simply run them off. The crossing of Indian Territory, north of the Red river, was paid for by gifts of cattle to the tribes. And in the north, the Kansas settlers were no more friendly than the Indians. The interests of cattlemen and farmer were bitterly opposed, and their struggle for supremacy was inevitable and bloody.

For the cowboys, the days were long and the work was hard. There was many a cow-hand who rubbed tobacco juice on his eyelids to keep awake. And when things went wrong, life was little better than hell. The diary of George Duffield, who drove 1000 longhorns right up to Iowa in 1866, recorded every sort of disaster: endless rain, several stampedes, violent thunderstorms, swollen rivers, Indian trouble, goods and food swept away, and a man drowned. 'Everything looks *blue* to me,' he complained, and no wonder. He hurt himself when his horse fell. He swam flooded rivers at night. He spent days chasing after stampeded cattle, going 60 hours without food or sleep. He dived under water to escape an enraged steer. He had to draw his gun to see off an ugly crowd of Indians. His back became

At the end of the trail was the railhead, from where the cattle were transported to Chicago and other northern centres of the meat trade. In this drawing longhorns are being driven out of the pens and into the railroad cars at one of the Kansas stockyards in the 1870s.

ABOVE When the drive was completed the cowboys were paid off – and proceeded to let their hair down. Russell's *In Without Knocking* is based on a specific incident, but this kind of behaviour was quite common on pay-day in any of the cow towns.

blistered and raw from summer sun. In October, after six months on the trail, he stumbled into his destination, Ottumwa (south-east of Des Moines), with fewer than half the cattle remaining. But when the cowboys heard the plaintive locomotive whistle out on the prairie and saw the tracks running into the clapboard shanties and false store-fronts of the cow-town, they whipped their ponies into a last tired gallop and went 'hallooing' into the dust and dirt of the Main Street.

'Like most of the boys,' said an old cowboy, 'I had to sow my wild oats, and I sowed all the money I made right along with the oats.' A cowboy on a cattle drive expected to make about 30 dollars a month. He was paid off at the railhead, and the town reckoned to take most of that money away from him before he took his sore head back to Texas. First, the cowboy bought some fancy clothes, bathed, and got a haircut. Then he was ready for the bartender, the faro dealer, and the 'calico queens' of the dance-

hall. His style was energetic and peculiar, wrote Joseph McCoy, 'with his huge spurs jingling at every step, his revolvers flapping up and down like a sheep's tail, and his eyes lit up with excitement, liquor, and lust'. Heated by drink, he passed his days in town between wildness and stupor. He was, said one observer, 'a species of centaur, half horse, half man, with immense spurs and dare-devil face'.

Cowtown Capers

The cattle town existed to help the cowboy have his fun and spend his money. Abilene (Kansas) was the first of them, and in its short reign of five years boasted 4 hotels, 10 rooming houses, 10 saloons, and 5 general stores, over all of which spread a dust cloud and the alarming stink of stockyard animals. There was also, down by the railway, an unsavoury shanty town. Abilene's glory was brief. By 1871 the biggest cattle drives had moved 100km (60 miles) westwards down the line to Ellsworth; then 145 km (90 miles) southwards to Wichita, and finally, around 1878, 225 km (140 miles) westwards to Dodge City (all in Kansas). Dodge had started as a mud hut beside a heap of buffalo hides, where the buffalo hunters who supplied meat for the railroad builders dumped their skins. For a few seasons it remained a frontier slum, but when the cattle arrived Dodge City suddenly blossomed into the grandest of all the cow-towns, with a reign that lasted into the late 1880s.

The cattle towns were wild places with a reputation for mayhem, but the amount of killing that went on there has been greatly exaggerated. The cowboy liked to be noisy with his gun, generally shooting at the sky and the stars, but he was rarely a wanton murderer. There were only 15 recorded murders in Dodge City in the 10 riotous years of its heyday. The desperadoes came, postured in the saloons, and left. The famous lawmen had little more to do than to kick drunks into the town jail. Yet a succession of great names in western myth passed through Abilene, Wichita, and Dodge. 'Bear River' Tom Smith was the first marshal of Abilene, an ex-New York cop who knocked out his opponents rather than shot them. He was followed by James Butler 'Wild Bill' Hickok, a slight, elegant man with ringlets down to his shoulders and a taste for silk shirts and fancy boots. He wore two pistols with ivory hilts and was known to be extremely fast on the draw. He had little trouble. Wyatt Earp began his career as deputy marshal in Wichita; he moved on to Dodge City after being fined for causing an affray.

Earp was an ex-buffalo hunter, as were such well-known western gunmen as Pat Garrett, 'Bat' Masterson, and William F. 'Buffalo Bill' Cody. These were the men who helped to wipe the buffalo off the Great Plains, providing meat for the railroad men, and hides for leather goods and industrial belting in the northern cities. Buffalo Bill, with his Springfield rifle nicknamed 'Lucretia Borgia', by his own reckoning killed 4280 buffalos in 17 months while contracting for the Kansas Pacific Railroad. Fortunately the deadly firepower of these men was less in evidence in the cattle towns. Dodge City might have been, as the hell-raisers claimed, 'a town with the hair on', but its cemetery filled up no more quickly than elsewhere. By 1881 Dodge had a reforming mayor, no liquor on Sundays, police in blue uniforms, and strict fines or even imprisonment for rowdiness.

The world of the cowboy and the cattle drive had grown up around a small number of tough, independent men. The first cattle ranchers were men of authority with vast spreads of land. Col. Samuel Maverick was so careless about his unbranded cattle that whenever a steer without a brand was caught the cry went up 'It's a maverick!' The colonel had a lordly attitude, and so too did his fellow owners. The giant 'Shanghai' Pierce used to greet his cattle from the low-lying Matagorda peninsula (Texas) with the shout, 'They're my sea-lions. They come right out of the Gulf of Mexico'. These were also men of power and possessions. At the

LEFT Even Dodge City, the widest open of the railhead towns, was a quiet little place on days when the cowboys and cattle were on the trail. This photograph was taken in the 1870s, when the town's prosperity was at its peak.

By 1880 the spread of the railways, the collapse of the market for longhorns, and the opening up of grasslands in the north spelt the death-knell of the great Texas cattle drives. The future lay with the farmers, such as this family of homesteaders posing outside their sod-house. By the end of the 19th century there were half a million farms on the great plains.

height of its success, Charles Goodnight's famous JA ranch in the Texas panhandle was worth over a million dollars. Yet Goodnight was a bit of a puritan and a bit of a crank. He banned drinking and gambling, and detested the innocent little cowboy game of mumblepeg, in which a knife was tossed so that its blade stuck in the ground.

The Coming of the Farmer

This free-wheeling world of aristocratic owners, tough cowboys, and stirring cattle drives did not last long. By 1880 the railway had penetrated deep into the South-West and there was no need for long trails. Range land was no longer unfenced and free. Land was being parcelled into lots of 65 ha (160 acres) and sold. Farming settlers were moving across the Missouri, planting arable crops. Corporations began to take over from the old cattle barons, buying up public land and fencing everyone off. 'They'll run a wire fence about Wyoming,' said one critic of the corporations, 'and everyone within will be notified to move.' Much of the new speculative money behind the cattle corporations was English, and it was said that the Rocking Chair Ranch used bloodhounds to round up the cattle.

The days of the longhorn trade were numbered. Improved breeds, specially Herefords, were brought into northern herds, and they were increasingly vulnerable to the splenic fever still carried by Texas longhorns. As beef prices for longhorns dropped in the South-West, the northern grasslands of Montana became available. Settlers and their fences encroached further and further on to the old range land. Two disastrous blizzards in 1884-5 and 1886-7 hit all western cattle, reducing numbers in some places by as much as 80 per cent. The open range where the cowboy roamed at will and got his living by skill with horse and lasso became a thing of the past. The new cowboy put wire on fence-posts and loaded hay off a wagon; he was just another farm-hand. But the old-timers shared memories of a roaring past, and they knew each other when they met. 'I would know,' wrote Teddy Blue, 'an old cowboy in hell with his hide burnt off. It's the way they stand and walk and talk.' The guns were laid up, and the arthritic legs could hardly get round a horse. 'But wherever they are is where I want to go.'

The future was with the farmers. The traditional pattern in Anglo-Saxon colonies had always placed farmers, not traders, at the frontier. For many years the settler with the plough resisted the Great Plains. He did not like the look of the treeless, wind-swept uplands. General William Tecumseh Sherman, writing from Colorado, suggested that only a government bounty, or necessity, would get people out there. But this great area of land was in the path of the western movement, and it was free.

As the older eastern land became exhausted by unrotated crops and emigrant thousands poured across the Missouri, the farmers decided to tread in the steps of the pioneers. The Homestead Act of 1862 offered settlers a free parcel of 65 ha (160 acres), which could be built up, under other legislation, to a freeholding of 195 ha (480 acres). New, struggling western communities, anxious for the security and prosperity that comes with more people, touted briskly for settlers. Kansas, said a local newspaper in 1867, had land as 'rich as that on the banks of the far-famed Nile'. The worthy senators of Dakota claimed, in 1869, that their state could grow anything from rye to buckwheat, from potatoes to melons. And when, in the 1870s, the railroad companies, with vast government land grants to dispose of, joined in the search for settlers, the din of propaganda was very loud indeed.

Slowly, the farmers came. With a wagon and family, with a few cattle and some domestic animals at their heels, they inched onto the plains. Without timber, they built sod-houses, dug into the ground and roofed with turf, which stayed cool in summer and warm in winter. They burnt brushwood or dried cow-dung; they dug a well, sometimes down to 30 m (100 ft), and hauled the water by hand. They ploughed and sowed a modest field, planting wheat mainly in the North and corn (maize) in the South. A kitchen garden gave vegetables for the household. The housewife made butter, cream, and cheese from the cows in the fenced pasture. Some hogs and poultry rooted around the house. It was a life full of disasters and labour. Sometimes drought came, sometimes storm. Crops failed, or were battered down, or were eaten by locusts. The Indians resented the settlers' advance, specially in that land which had been Indian Territory. Cattlemen cut the settlers' fences, trampled their crops, and horse-whipped the protesters. Then perhaps the settler would hitch up the wagon again, leave that dreary patch, and plod on westward.

Always there was work – endless, backbreaking labour. 'Done my housework, then made fried cakes, squash pies, baked wheat bread and corn bread, cut out a night-dress and partly made it,' wrote a Kansas farmer's wife in 1873; 'am very tired'. She had the children, the animals, and the vegetable garden to care for as well. And her husband, often single-handed, built and dug and irrigated and ploughed and sowed and reaped, all for an income that might not exceed more than 150 dollars a year.

But the optimists were right. Although the country was difficult, the endurance of the plains farmer, with some help from improving agricultural science, made the land pay off. By 1900 there were more than 500,000 farms on the Great Plains producing 185 million bushels of grain, one third of the total American output. It was a remarkable success story. The bleak wilderness that had been condemned by so many early travellers became, in less than a century, the granary of the world.

The Wilderness Tamed

*As the western settlements grew in size and
prosperity the need arose for lines of fast
and reliable communication with the older states
back east. By the late 1850s the way was open for the
first continental stage-coach service . . . .*

A settled land needs transport and good communications; these are the veins and arteries along which the economic life-blood flows. In the West, by the mid-19th century, the pioneer mountain man had given way to the permanent settler. Emigrants were filling the land. The census of 1850 revealed that the population of the western territories was approaching 250,000. The old ramshackle paths of trade and travel were no longer good enough to supply and maintain a booming economy. For the success of the West, for the safety of the expanding nation, and to encourage development of a sense of unity, broad highways were needed to bind the ambitious new order in the West to the old society of the east coast.

And, of course, there was profit to be made. Public needs could be satisfied for the benefit of private gain. 'American society,' a European commented, 'is not so much a democracy as a huge commercial company for the discovery, cultivation, and capitalization of its enormous territory.' But from the beginning the new lands had been a playground for free enterprise. A government that gave nothing more than a few concessions needed private initiative to build public works.

Before the stampede of the Forty-niners it was clear that Oregon and California required new routes. In the late 1840s there was even talk of a transcontinental railroad. In 1848 John Charles Frémont, that tireless promoter of western interests, looked for new passes without success. At the same time, the Army lent a hand, and Capt Howard Stansbury pioneered a good trail over the Cheyenne Pass and into Laramie (Wyoming). But the means were not yet available to tackle the gigantic undertaking of the railway line. Better communications between East and West began on a more modest scale with the search for a reliable mail service.

In 1850 the well-organized Mormon community in Utah began an irregular service, carrying mail by coach between Salt Lake City and Independence, the trail terminus on the Missouri. The journey, which was slow and always subject to long delays, stopped entirely when the anti-Mormon feeling in the United States spilled over into active hostility. With this traffic cut off, California was isolated once more. In 1856 the angry citizens of the fastest-growing state petitioned Congress for a decent wagon-road to the East and a daily mail service. A

OPPOSITE A stage-coach stops for a change of horses at a lonely way-station in California, allowing the cramped passengers to get out and stretch their legs. Carl William Hahn painted this scene in 1875, six years after the coast-to-coast railroad was completed: the coach would provide long-distance transport in remote areas for many years yet.

BELOW A fully loaded Concord coach. Expensive but strong and comfortable, these iron and ashwood coaches took their name from the New Hampshire town where they were built.

Frederic Remington's *Coming and Going of the Pony Express* shows the split-second timing in the relay of horses and riders on which the speed of this celebrated but short-lived mail service depended. The mail was carried in a Mexican *mochila*, with four lockable pockets, seen on the saddle of the departing pony at left.

year later Congress authorised a service for passengers and mail between the Mississippi and San Francisco, in 'good four-horse coaches', each journey to be completed within 25 days.

The Overland Mail

The contract was awarded to the New Yorker John Butterfield, an imposing figure whose energy matched his large size. Competing interests had handed him a poor route, 4500 km (2795 miles) from St Louis (Missouri) to San Francisco via El Paso (Texas), Tucson (Arizona), and Los Angeles. He had one year to survey the route, build the stations, buy the coaches, hire the staff, and arrange for

supplies. Butterfield, in yellow cloak and broad-brimmed hat, was everywhere. 'He is,' wrote an admiring reporter, 'the most energetic president I ever saw.' He built 141 stage posts. He cleared tracks, put up bridges, and dug wells. He bought 250 Concord and Celerity coaches and 1800 horses and mules to pull them. He hired a host of drivers, grooms, liverymen, blacksmiths, managers, and agents. The cost of a through ticket was 200 dollars and shorter journeys were rated at 10 cents a mile. In September 1858 Butterfield was ready, and on the 16th he took the train to Tipton (mid-way between St Louis and Independence), where the rail line ended. Here he stepped into the first coach

premiums above the regular fare. An Englishman making the journey in 1860 reported such a crush in the coach that they had to sit with 'tightly dovetailed knees', while an indefinite number clung to the outside: 'by popular permission, an American vehicle is never "full"'. In this discomfort they jolted over plains and mountains, and across deserts where the route-markers were piles of bleached bones. Choked on dust, and with bodies too racked and aching for sleep, they grabbed meals in dim adobe houses and hurried on lest the Apache overtook them. But twice a week, in both directions, in duststorm and snowstorm, the mail coaches got through, and Butterfield prospered.

The Pony Express

Soon other freighters cast envious eyes on Butterfield's success. The old partnership of William Hepburn Russell, Alexander Majors, and William Waddell had grown rich, first as wagoners on the Santa Fe Trail, then as suppliers to Army outposts. By 1858 they ran 3500 wagons and 40,000 oxen, and were worth some 2 million dollars. That was enough for Majors and Waddell, but scheming Will Russell was not satisfied. At the end of 1859, having lost money on a Colorado coach venture, he proposed to cut into Butterfield's business by starting a rapid mail service using fast horses. He bought expensive mounts and advertised for 'Young, skinny, wiry fellows not over 18. Must be expert riders willing to risk death daily. Orphans preferred'. Two of the many youngsters who applied were the 15-year-old William F. Cody, later famous as Buffalo Bill, and the slightly older James Butler (Wild Bill) Hickok, who got a job as a stage-post hand.

Armed with a bible 'to defend himself against moral contamination' and a pair of Colt revolvers, the first Pony Express rider spurred his black horse out of St Joseph (Missouri) at 5 pm on 3 April 1860. The journey to Sacramento in California, using 75 ponies in relay, took 10½ days; the cost for letters was 10 dollars per ounce. The riders kept up a fierce pace and reckoned to get through come what may. Bill Cody claimed that he once rode 21 hours without relief and covered 515 km (320 miles). A service so swift and dedicated should have been a success. But although the Pony Express could outspeed Butterfield, it could not leave science behind. As the riders criss-crossed the continent at a gallop they flashed past small groups of workmen, advancing at a sedate pace, sinking poles into the ground: the transcontinental telegraph was pushing forward, at the rate of about 19 km (12 miles) a day, converging from east and west on Salt Lake City. On 24 October 1861 the wires were connected and the first message instantaneously joined coast to coast. Two days later, the Pony Express died. Lamented the Sacramento *Bee*: 'a senseless, soulless thing that eats not, sleeps not, tires not, has encompassed, overthrown and routed you'. In 18

of the Butterfield Overland Mail, accompanied by two mail-sacks, three passengers, and a newspaper reporter. Butterfield's son, resplendent in an enormous checked bow-tie, cracked the whip, and the California service was underway.

Just after sunrise on Sunday, 10 October, the coach rolled triumphantly – and ahead of schedule – into San Francisco. By this enterprise, said the exultant *Bulletin*, 'California is bound to the rest of the Union'. Within a short time the service had become a great success. It proved itself reliable, and it was far easier than the alarming sea-passage around Cape Horn. Butterfield reduced his prices, and the passengers fought for places, offering large

months Russell, Majors, and Waddell had lost 200,000 dollars on the Pony Express.

In the same year disaster overtook the Butterfield Mail. The Civil War broke out, the South withdrew from the Union, and the southerly stage coach route was blocked. Congress anxiously wanted the riches of California, so the mail coaches were re-routed to the north, following roughly the line of the Pony Express. But John Butterfield was ageing and tired, and he allowed his business to pass into the needy hands of Will Russell. The northern service was established, but it could not rescue Russell. His large business gradually sank in a bog of debt and deceit, until it was plucked out of his control by the unscrupulous hand of Ben Holladay.

An ex-saloon keeper and whiskey distiller with a sharp eye for any kind of profit, Holladay had a financial stranglehold on the debt-ridden Russell. In March 1862 the black-bearded, cold-blooded Holladay, known to be 'wholly destitute of honesty, morality, or common decency', called in his mortgage and inherited at a stroke the major part of western traffic.

For a few years the renamed Holladay Overland Mail prospered. The man now called the Stagecoach King played poker and waited, watching the development of the West. He patrolled his empire in a Concord coach with reading lamps and a built-in bar, and pulled by a team of matching horses. When Indians troubled him he sent for the Army to punish them. His success was great, and soon the rich and powerful eye of Wells, Fargo & Co was attracted to his business. Holladay played along with this powerful California transport firm because

LEFT A trainload of 30 brand-new Concord coaches en route to Wells, Fargo's depot at Omaha (Nebraska) in April 1868. Each door of each of these coaches had a different scene painted on it by J. Burgum, who also painted this picture.

INSET A logging train crosses a timber trestle bridge during construction of one of the transcontinental railroads. Vast areas of forest were cleared to provide the timber for such bridges, for the ties (sleepers) – and for the old wood-burning locomotives.

he had noted the uneven but inevitable advance of the railroad. In 1866 he judged it was time to sell; and Wells' Fargo, who still reckoned on a few more years of profitable stagecoach monopoly, bought the business. Once again Holladay proved himself to be more astute than his rivals: the trains arrived as quickly as he had foreseen. He got out a rich man, while Wells' Fargo watched the locomotives ride over their dying business.

Rails Across the Continent

The railroad had come to the West in a modest way in 1856, when Theodore Judah had built a little line from Sacramento to the nearby goldfields. Judah was not satisfied by this. He had a grand vision of his track extending eastwards, crossing mountains and plains to the Mississippi. Lobbying for his dream in

Central Pacific gangers, at work on the western section of the first transcontinental railroad, lay an arrow-straight length of track across the Nevada desert in 1868 where the Chinese labourers once laid 16km (10 miles) in a day.

Washington and California, Judah persuaded a grocer, a dry-goods merchant, and two hardware men to form a company, and they became the Big Four of the Central Pacific Railroad. By 1862 Congress was convinced of the value of a transcontinental line, and on 1 July President Abraham Lincoln signed an Act for its completion. Two companies were authorised to build it, one starting from California and the other from the eastern side of the Great Plains. The government promised a loan for construction varying in amount from 16,000 dollars a mile on the plains to 48,000 dollars a mile in the mountains. In addition, the two companies – the Central Pacific in the West and the Union Pacific in the East – were granted 2600 ha (6400 acres) of public land for each completed mile of track. In return the government gained a concessionary rate on the line for all its business.

Both sides thought they had a bargain. The government, by the issue of some bonds, by the gift of public land, and by tearing up or simply ignoring its Indian treaties, would promote a valuable public asset. The directors of the railroads confidently expected to make a fortune. The close-knit clique of controlling shareholders who ran the two companies quickly saw that there was more plunder in constructing the line than there was revenue in operating it. By financial juggling and downright fraud, they diverted vastly inflated profits from construction contracts into their own pockets. The rewards for corruption were very large. A later investigation of the Crédit Mobilier, which was the Union Pacific front-company, put the figure at a minimum of 23 million dollars and perhaps as high as 100 million dollars. The Contract and Finance Co, behind which hid the Central Pacific, was harder to investigate: it just so happened that its records had disappeared in a fire! But the Big Four did not starve: Leland Stanford and Collie Huntington became household names in California; Charley

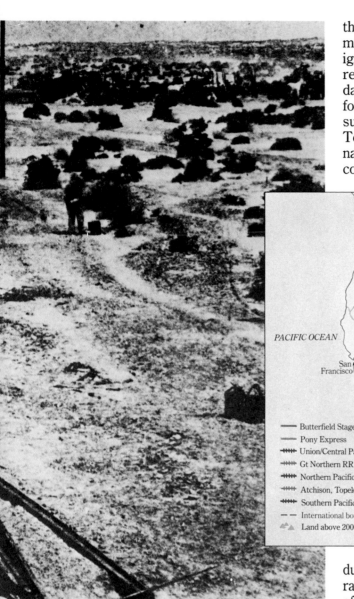

the builders explained, meant that 'the locomotive must go forward; and it is in vain that these poor ignorant creatures attempt to stay its progress by resisting inch by inch'. No doubt it was with Indian danger in mind that Thomas Durant, the driving force behind Union Pacific, set out to enlist the support of the Civil War hero General William Tecumseh Sherman. In 1865, seated on a keg of nails, the general rode a flatcar on the few miles of completed track and was entertained with roast

duck and good French wine. Sherman became a railroad enthusiast – even more so when he was offered at a discount, and purchased, a large parcel of land from the Union Pacific holding.

'Never before,' wrote a visiting Englishman, 'has hostility to the pale-face raged so fiercely in the hearts of the Indians.' Seeing their treaties violated, their lands bisected by the iron horse, and their stock of buffalo nearly wiped out for hungry railmen, the warlike Sioux were in ferment. Once again the U.S. Army was persuaded of its duty to make the plains safe for trains and profitmaking.

In 1866 a Sioux and Cheyenne war-party trapped and killed 81 soldiers. Construction workers were frightened to go on, and Durant demanded more action. Sherman replied energetically, insisting that the Indians 'must die or submit to our dictation'. Many died, but chose to go down fighting. They derailed trains, fought a guerrilla campaign against soldiers, ambushed and harried gangs of workmen. For the labourers, a gun became as handy a tool as a pick. Sherman had to take the matter seriously, and to safeguard the railroad he built forts and organized friendly Pawnee Indians into mercenary companies commanded by U.S. Army officers – all this at the taxpayers' expense.

Map of U.S. transcontinental communications in the second half of the 19th century. The railways shown represent the coast-to-coast lines in about 1880.

Crocker, ex-dry goods man, left 24 million dollars, and Mark Hopkins, ex-hardware man, about 19 million dollars.

No wonder, then, that the speaker at the Union Pacific ground-breaking ceremony in Omaha (Nebraska) in December 1863 should have called the transcontinental railroad 'the grandest enterprise under God'. But although extraordinary riches were anticipated, the line had to be built nonetheless, and that posed some problems.

To begin with, there was bound to be trouble with Indians. A good part of the huge acreage so graciously donated to the railways was stolen from Indian land solemnly guaranteed by government treaty. The Grand Excursion, which the Union Pacific organized in 1866 to impress the New York money men, picnicked on the 100th meridian, not caring that this was already 400 km (250 miles) inside the line promised to the Indians as their 'permanent frontier'. The laws of civilization, one of

The Golden Spike ceremony, at which the Central Pacific (left) and Union Pacific rail tracks were joined, took place at Promontory Point (Utah) on 10 May 1869. Poorly built in many sections and financed by dubious methods, the completed railroad was nonetheless a powerful symbol of Americans' growing sense of the unity of East and West.

Under threat from the Indians, and struggling with difficulties of organization and construction, the progress of the line was slow at first. In the East two whole years were given to grading. The first rail was not laid until 10 July 1865, and the first mile took 11 days. By the end of November the track was still only 48 km (30 miles) west of the Missouri. In the West the problems were rather different. The Central Pacific had little trouble from Indians, and their route was shorter, being 1194 km (742 miles) against the 1670 (1038 miles) to be built by the eastern company. But the mountains of the Sierra Nevada sat huge and forbidding in the way of the Central Pacific, which had to transport rails and heavy equipment by ship around the Horn.

The work in the mountains was hard and dangerous, and the labourers, at 2 dollars a day, did not stay long. To overcome the discontents and bloody-mindedness of the white labour force, the Central Pacific tried an experiment with Chinese workmen. The results were good. The Chinese, though small, were tough, industrious, and uncomplaining. Best of all for the company, they would work for a dollar a day. Soon Charley Crocker had arranged a regular flow of workers from China, men who spoke no English and were completely dependent on the goodwill of the company. Moving in mass, in blue smocks, they shifted millions of cubic feet of mountainside with pick, shovel, and wheelbarrow. After such a slow beginning, the race to the meeting point was on: Chinese labourers moving mountains in the west and American gangers spurting across the Great Plains from the east.

In 1866 the Union Pacific shrewdly put their track-laying in the hands of the Casement brothers, who contracted to do the job for 750 dollars a mile. General Jack Casement and his young brother Dan, little men with full beards, were whirlwinds of energy: they were described as 'a pair of the biggest little men you ever saw – about as large as 12-year-old boys, but requiring larger hats'. General Jack was the boss, a taskmaster who drove his motley crews of Irishmen, Civil War veterans, and 'Galvanized Yanks' like a little tyrant, while brother Dan, a wizard with numbers, looked after equipment and supplies. They put together a special train which followed in the steps of the builders and provided most of their wants. There were dorm-itory cars, kitchen and eating cars, a wash-house, shops for blacksmiths, carpenters and tool-makers, even a telegraph office. This was accompan-ied by an unofficial rabble of camp-followers who were staked out on the plain and provided other services. Here were the card dealers, the buffalo slaughterers, the sellers of raw liquor.

Under the Casements the work swung along to the sound of raucous singing and rhythmic blows of the hammer. 'It is a grand anvil chorus, three strokes to the spike', wrote one observer. 'There are ten spikes to a rail, 400 rails to a mile, 1800 miles to San Francisco – 21 million times are those sledges to be swung.' Incentive payments spurred the gangs on: a pound of tobacco a man for a mile in a day, and a wage and a half for a mile and a half in a day. By the end of 1866 the Casement crews had managed 105 km (65 miles) in a month up the gentle valley of the Platte. The following year the Union Pacific was approaching the Wasatch range of the Rockies; the Central Pacific was out of the Sierras and starting across the dry desert of Nevada, on the level surface of which the tireless Chinese once achieved 16 km (10 miles) in a day. The rivalry of the race was whipped up in each camp and trumpeted by newspapers around the nation. The graders on each side, well in advance of the tracklayers, hurrying on from dug-out to dug-out burrowed in the ground, met and elbowed each other for the best route, brawling and attacking with blasting powder. In 1869 Congress had to settle the squab-ble and chose Promontory Point, just to the north of the Great Salt Lake, as the place where the con-verging tracks would join.

Early in May 1869 the chief men of the two

Fanny Palmer's *Across the Continent* (1868), one of the most popular prints of its time, celebrates the pioneer spirit. It shows a small, hard-working community, with its own church and school, winning a good living from the western wilderness. The coast-to-coast railway links the settlement with the rest of the country – and the peaceable Indians keep their distance on the other side of the tracks.

OPPOSITE Frederic Remington's *The Quest* shows a detachment of the U.S. Cavalry on assignment in the South-West. Too often in the latter part of the century the Cavalry's role was to enforce the government's unjust policies against the Indians, whose lands and rights were whittled away by the tide of westward migration.

RIGHT A Union Pacific poster announces the opening of the first scheduled railroad service to the Pacific from the East. The journey from Omaha, on the Missouri, to San Francisco took less than four days. Suddenly, the continent seemed to have shrunk.

companies journeyed to Utah for the joining ceremony. Durant, of the Union Pacific, was delayed by angry workmen who chained his railcar to the line until they were paid. This was one occasion when Durant did not argue. He sent for the paymaster and hurried up the line for the feast and the speeches. At Promontory Point, on 10 May, the link was made. 'A gap of only one rail remained,' wrote a wood hauler on the Central Pacific, 'and the bedding and laying of that was done with much ceremony. The last tie was of laurel handsomely ornamented. It

1869. **May 10th.** 1869.
GREAT EVENT
Rail Road from the Atlantic to the Pacific
GRAND OPENING
— OF THE —
Union Pacific
RAIL ROAD,
PLATTE VALLEY ROUTE.
PASSENGER TRAINS LEAVE
OMAHA
ON THE ARRIVAL OF TRAINS FROM THE EAST.
THROUGH TO SAN FRANCISCO
In less than Four Days, avoiding the Dangers of the Sea!
Travelers for Pleasure, Health or Business
Will find a Trip over The Rocky Mountains Healthy and Pleasant.
LUXURIOUS CARS & EATING HOUSES
ON THE UNION PACIFIC RAIL ROAD.
PULLMAN'S PALACE SLEEPING CARS
RUN WITH ALL THROUGH PASSENGER TRAINS.
GOLD, SILVER AND OTHER MINERS!
Now is the time to seek your Fortunes in Nebraska, Wyoming, Arizona, Washington, Dakotah Colorado, Utah, Oregon, Montana, New Mexico, Idaho, Nevada or California.
CONNECTIONS MADE AT
CHEYENNE for DENVER, CENTRAL CITY & SANTA FE
AT OGDEN AND CORINNE FOR HELENA, BOISE CITY, VIRGINIA CITY, SALT LAKE CITY AND ARIZONA.
THROUGH TICKETS FOR SALE AT ALL PRINCIPAL RAILROAD OFFICES!
Be Sure they Read via Platte Valley or Omaha
Company's Office 72 La Salle St., opposite City Hall and Court House Square, Chicago.
CHARLES E. NICHOLS, Ticket Agent.
G. P. GILMAN, JOHN P. HART, J. BUDD, W. SNYDER,

was laid and two gold and two silver spikes were driven.' Stanford of the Central Pacific wielded the ceremonial sledge, and was jeered when he missed his stroke. It was a bright, cold day and the officials soon retired to the Central Pacific cars, where 'whiskey flowed abundantly and seemed to be the chief attraction'.

Raised on corruption and built with too much haste by labour that was partly forced and partly bribed, the transcontinental line was only just serviceable. The government inspector was not impressed. Noting that the completion was seven years ahead of schedule, he commented that 'this may be American enterprise, or it may be American recklessness'. He thought that the public and the nation had been badly swindled, for the gifts offered to the promoters by way of 'subsidies and lands were too great for poor, avaricious human nature to resist'. And now the public, having mightily contributed through the government to the enrichment of a handful of rogues, had the privilege of paying yet further for passage over a doubtful track.

The first dreamers of the transcontinental railroad had prophesied that emigrants would rush along it: 'Ten million of emigrants will settle in this golden land within twenty years,' wrote one. And further benefits would follow; they saw the line as a channel of opportunity, bringing life to a land that was previously barren. As the speech-maker had said when the first clod of earth was turned on that winter day in Omaha, the Pacific railway was 'at the entrance of a garden 700 miles in length and 20 broad'.

Despite the fraud and the shoddy construction, the line did live up to the dreams of the faithful. It was the necessary tie that pulled together the halves of America. With the ease and the convenience of the rail journey, the West ceased to be the frontier and became a familiar part of the body of the nation. Other coast-to-coast lines were soon being built: the Great Northern and the Northern Pacific between the Union Pacific and the Canadian border; the Atchison, Topeka & Santa Fe to Los Angeles via Kansas City and Santa Fe; and the Southern Pacific from New Orleans to Los Angeles via Houston, El Paso, and Yuma. These lines were also troubled by fraud and financial manipulation, by misuse of land grants and exploitation of workers. A few millionaires established monopoly powers, which they practised without conscience. But the fingers of steel stretched throughout the West and brought a glow of prosperity wherever they touched. The mule and the horse had opened the West, plodding and stumbling under explorers, fur traders, and mountain men. The iron horse at last burst into that opening, tireless, punctual, almost unstoppable. With its speed, power, capacity, and reliability it cancelled barriers and made the whole nation one land.

An American Tragedy

*The westward migration was heedless of the rights of
the Indians whose settlements lay in its path.
The 'manifest destiny' of the white man
meant the disinheritance of the Indians – but
not before an era of violence had
taken a dreadful toll....*

The simple rule of conquest, which aggressive nations have followed since the beginning of time, is that the defeated must submit or die. The Europeans did not go to North America out of benevolence or charity towards the native Indians: they went to make better lives for themselves. The raw facts of their new life as they struggled for space and fortune in a strange country meant that they would override, if they had to, native lands, native law, native custom, native peace, and native lives.

In the first days of settlement before 1800, when the east coast states were growing up, white man and red man co-existed uneasily. The newcomers needed the old inhabitants to show the way in the wilderness, to help them survive, to be allies in European wars, and to be customers for the white man's goods. But inevitably, as American power expanded, so Indian power contracted. The land-hunger of a growing population forced the Indian tribes westward. Those Indians who resisted were driven out by arms. Those who had accepted the whites and aped their ways, yet still wanted to keep their lands, were undone by fraud and violence. The Cherokee, one of the so-called Five Civilized Tribes, were forced out of their peaceful, developing community in Georgia and sent west on their 'Trail of Tears', on which some 4000 of them died.

Once across the Mississippi, the Indians stopped and resettled. The incoming tribes had to fight for their place against the Plains Indians, but the land was wide and full of buffalo. There was room for all. After a while, though the tribes skirmished and fought, territories were staked out and Indian life went on without much interference from the white man. It seemed that the white man was content to leave it like this. Thomas Jefferson had thought that the Mississippi might be a good and natural boundary for Indian lands. The first explorers of the Great Plains, finding the country very unattractive and unsuitable for emigrant farmers, thought it a fine dumping ground for Indians. Zebulon Pike, in 1807, suggested that pioneers 'leave the prairies . . . to the wandering and uncivilised aborigines . . .'.

As far as the whites were concerned Indians were 'savages' and the white man's civilization took precedence over their ancient rights. If they were allowed to exist, they did so under licence and at the whim of a 'superior' people. Yet when the westward migration began to flow, after the Louisiana Purchase of 1800, the emigrants could hardly move a step at first without Indian help. Meriwether Lewis and William Clark frequently relied on Indians to guide them, help them, and rescue them on their journey from 1804 to 1806. The trail-blazing mountain men would not have lasted six months in the wilderness without Indian advice, Indian habits, Indian friends, and Indian wives. Tribes like the Nez Percé and the Flatheads practically nursed the pioneers through the first years of endurance in the mountains of the north-west.

The general opinion was that Indians were there to be used. They might have disgusting habits, eating dog and putrid meat, but they showed the white man the valuable roots and grasses of the land and taught the art of preserving wind-dried meat. Their simple economy and lack of trade and industry were derided by white men, but the early success of the fur trade depended on Indian knowledge of the beaver and its habits.

Since the white man wanted more and more of the riches of the land, the Indian, who was content with modest rewards, was to be driven to it. The Sioux, who had rather inefficiently ferried the furs from the mountains to the river traders, angrily found themselves cut out by the fur companies. Those Indians who were too lazy (in the white view) or too unambitious to feed the coffers of white civilization were cunningly plied with alcohol, for which the Indians developed a fatal weakness. 'Gave them ¼ glass of whiskey,' Clark wrote in

1804 at a tricky meeting on the river, 'which they appeared to be very fond of. Sucked the bottles after it was out and soon began to be troublesome.' Drink was a dangerous drug for the Indians. It made them confused, wild, and unreliable. But it made them dependent on the white man, and in this submissive state they could be forged into what Meriwether Lewis called 'a very necessary link in the chain which is to unite these nations and ourselves in a state of commercial intercourse'.

The wiser chiefs knew that relations with the white man that were based on greed, exploitation and the destruction of native culture were unsound. 'We are now killing the beaver without any labour,' said one, 'we are now rich, but shall soon be poor, for when the beaver are destroyed we have nothing to depend on.' But what were the chiefs to do? Year by year, more and more emigrants poured over the Mississippi and the Missouri. Even before the headlong rush at the mid-century, Narcissa Whit-

man had concluded in the 1840s that white new-comers pressed too hard on the Indian population, and her experienced missionary husband later judged that the Indian was doomed: 'it is equally useless to oppose or desire it otherwise'.

Nor did the wisest chiefs have the organization or authority either to check the immigration or to force just terms out of the white man. Each tribe was independent and democratic, and the chief was obeyed only so far as it pleased his tribesmen. The horse Indians of the Great Plains, in particular, were warrior societies, always at war with their neighbours and rivals. It was easy for sharp Americans to divide them and rule, to set one tribal group against another. They could always find some disgruntled chief to make a treaty, to 'cede' land according to a document which the Indians neither understood nor meant to obey. And later, by the same token, the whites seldom hesitated to renounce treaties they found inconvenient.

The life of many Plains Indians centred upon the vast migrating herds of buffalo. The shaggy monsters provided them not only with food but also with materials for clothing, shelter, and much else. The white man gained control over the free-roaming Plains peoples partly by subduing them in battle and partly by wiping out the buffalo.

INSET Europeans and Indians were not always at loggerheads. The early trappers relied on the help of friendly Indian pathfinders in the mountains, and the fur companies often welcomed Indian trappers, as here, at their trading posts.

White Man Against Red

In the West, specially on the Great Plains and in the foothills of the Rockies, settler and Indian came head to head. Their interests could not be reconciled. The kindly men of the US Indian Bureau hoped that the Indians would settle down and become farmers, like white men. But the tribes had rootless, wandering blood in the veins and became angry and desperate when their ranges and their buffaloes began to disappear. They were demoralized, too, by drink and by such European gifts as smallpox, cholera, measles, scrofula, and syphilis. The gold-rush and the hordes that followed it after 1849 overwhelmed them, and they seemed likely to revert to that 'savagery' of which they had always been accused.

Irritation burst out into short, bloody conflicts. Indians waylaid innocent travellers and murdered them. White men shot unsuspecting Indians out of hand. Injustice rankled. Mojave Indians, who had been attacked by James Pattie in 1826, took revenge on Jed Smith's expedition in 1827. The Army

RIGHT Remington's celebrated *A Dash for the Timber* is one of his many paintings that depict the fierce hostility between the Plains Indians and the cowboys hired by the cattle barons, whose ranches fenced off vast areas of what had been the Indians' traditional hunting grounds.

was drawn more and more into the West, not so much to keep the peace as to punish Indians, who came to be regarded everywhere as hostile. 'We, the military,' General Sherman wrote, 'charged with a general protection of the infant settlements and long routes of travel, have to dispose our troops and act as if they [the Indians] were hostile.'

Between the gold-rush and the Civil War, the Army had trouble with the Sioux, the Arapaho, the Cheyenne, and the Comanche, all quick-tempered and aggressive peoples. In 1862 the Santee Sioux broke out in Minnesota. A fracas that began with the theft of some eggs led to an unprovoked slaughter of white settlers and a merciless reprisal from the white militia. The country was left desolate, the white farms abandoned, and the Santee were hanged or driven out. In 1864, in Colorado, a misunderstanding over cattle thefts put the tribes in tumult and caused the soldiers, under the murderous ex-preacher Col. John Chivington, to go Indian hunting. After several cruel little episodes, Chivington and the Third Colorado Cavalry fell on the

unsuspecting Cheyenne people of Chief Black Kettle, who were camped with 100 lodges and some 500 women and children on the dry bed of Sand Creek, some 260 km (162 miles) south-east of Denver. At dawn, on 29 November, they attacked the unguarded camp and killed 163 Indians, of whom 110 were women and children. 'Colorado soldiers,' boasted a Denver newspaper, 'have once again covered themselves with glory.' Nearby, a small township retains the dubious distinction of being named after Chivington.

After the Sand Creek massacre, and with the ending of the Civil War, Indian relations in the West moved into a state of crisis. A Congressional committee reported in 1867 that the Indians were losing numbers fast owing to disease, drunkenness, war, and starvation. Their homelands on the Great Plains were being overrun by white adventurers who thought nothing of exterminating red men. The advancing rail lines were cutting off the routes of the buffalo herds, which were being slaughtered in any case by white hunters. The paternal policies of the Indian Bureau, to buy off Indians with annuities or to persuade them into reservations, were not working. The Indian took to the white man's vices easily enough, but not to the virtues of stability, hard work, and profitable enterprise. There was, the committee sadly concluded, an 'irrepressible conflict between a superior and an inferior race'. To all those Americans who believed in 'manifest destiny' this was hardly surprising. 'The truth is,' wrote the missionary Jason Lee, expressing the white man's view of the native struggle, 'they are *Indians.*'

In 1865, released from the battlefields of the Civil War and perhaps brutalized by the terrible carnage they had seen there, more and more soldiers were sent to the West. They, as well as the civilians, could see the bloodstained road down which the Indians were going. 'We shall in a few years have before us,' Col. Marcy wrote in 1866, 'the alternative of exterminating them or fighting them perpetually.' To the soldiers the problem of the West was a military problem only, to be resolved by armies in the normal way, and they wanted a free hand in dealing with it. General Sherman wrote to General Philip Sheridan about bringing 'the Indian problem to a final solution'.

Sherman wanted to create a 600 km (375 mile) wide belt of plains between the Platte and the Arkansas rivers that was free of all Indians, and a line of forts established from Fort Laramie in eastern Wyoming north-westward to the Montana goldfields. Old Jim Bridger, the Indians' friend, laid out a trail that avoided the valued Indian country on the Powder river, east of the Bighorn Mountains of northern Wyoming. But the trader John Bozeman drove right through these hunting grounds, because of their excellent grazing. The Sioux were prepared to allow a passage to emigrants who did no damage, but they would not tolerate the Army on their favourite range. In July 1866 they made their warning clear by killing some soldiers at Crazy Woman's Creek, a tributary of the Powder river. In December Capt. William Fetterman led a larger company along the same trial. Sioux and Cheyenne braves under Red Cloud ambushed this company near Fort Phil Kearny, killing 81 soldiers. General Sherman vowed a revenge on behalf of the Army: 'We must act with vindictive earnestness against the Sioux, even to their extermination'.

The Cavalry Offensive

There was a lull before the last contest. Many in the government had sympathy for the Indians, and they wanted to try peace before the military were let loose. A peace commission, which did not please the generals, agreed to set aside two large Indian preserves: the Indian Territory of Kansas in the south, and most of the Dakotas in the north, from the Missouri southwards, across the Yellowstone, and on to the upper Powder river country. But in the independent world of the tribesmen, treaties made by some chiefs had no effect on others. Comanches, Kiowas, Arapahoes, and southern Cheyennes insisted on their immemorial right to hunt where they pleased. Furthermore, several tribes had a history of hatred towards the whites. The turbulent Comanches had always regarded any Texan as fair game, and other Indians were eager to avenge the Sand Creek massacre. Throughout 1868 a nasty

little war of attrition was fought around the Kansas reservation. The southern tribes were dangerously stirred up, plundering, burning and sometimes raping. The Army attempted to impose strict control on the reservation, while the soldiers prepared for a winter campaign in the south. 'These Indians require to be soundly whipped,' said General Sheridan, 'and the ringleaders . . . hung, their ponies killed, and such destruction of their property as will make them very poor.'

In the autumn, Jim Bridger came to Fort Hays (the present Hays, Kansas), on arthritic legs and with dimming eyes. From the depth of his profound experience, gained in more than 40 years of western pioneering, he begged the Army to drop its war-plan. But Sheridan would not listen. In November 1868 George A. Custer, with flowing flaxen hair and an unhealthy thirst for glory (he took along a tame newspaper reporter as his guest), led the 7th Cavalry out of Fort Hays, looking to make a military reputation against near-naked enemies on bare horseback.

Indian fighting was not an easy matter, however, for the ordinary U.S. cavalryman faced an enemy who tested his courage and endurance to the full. The Indian brave lived for war, and he was mobile, cunning, and well-armed. He was a sharp tactician and he knew the country. He could outride the Yankees, and probably outlast them too. But Indian warfare had fatal weaknesses. Obviously the raw

Sioux braves attacking Custer's forces at the Battle of the Little Bighorn.

military power of the whites was formidable, with cannons, howitzers, machine guns, strong forts, secure and plentiful supplies. Beyond that the Indians were unable to combine, they were subject to vicious ancient rivalries, with one tribe always willing to deal treacherously with another. Warfare was also a seasonal business, which packed up for the winter. And the Indian in his winter quarters, unprotected in flimsy lodges with his chattels, wives, and children around him, was an easy mark for disciplined forces on a winter campaign.

Custer led the 7th Cavalry through the early snows to the Indian camp on the Washita (near the Canadian river in Oklahoma). There, they fell upon Black Kettle's Cheyennes, killing 103 Indians and 875 horses, burning the lodges and taking into captivity Indian women and children. This was the start of a six-year campaign against the southern tribes of Cheyenne, Kiowas and Comanches. General Sheridan was an unforgiving foe. It was he who coined the inglorious phrase that 'the only good Indian is a dead Indian'. And with ambitious daredevils like Custer to carry out Sheridan's plans, by 1875 the southern tribes were beaten. The most dangerous leaders were gaoled in Florida. The tribes were penned into the Kansas reservation and denied finally their freedom of the Great Plains.

In the north, the fragile peace agreed in 1868 held up for a few years. Many Indians reported to the agency on the reservation, which attempted to turn them, with no great success, from nomadic hunters into American farmers. But the Sioux confederacy in general distrusted and avoided the white man, and the Hunkpapa Sioux chief Sitting Bull in particular tried to carry on the old Indian life within the range the government had allowed him. But agreements made by government in Washington had little effect on frontier people. The emigrants, the prospectors, the settlers saw no reason why the Indians should keep a large chunk of the best western land. Then, in 1874, Sheridan and Custer, that established team of Indian hunters, moved their operations from the southern to the northern plains. Custer led the 7th Cavalry into the Black Hills of South Dakota, into territory which was sacred ground of the Sioux nation.

There was some trickery about this expedition, for it is not clear whether Custer went to harry the Indians or to search for gold (he led a military party with geologists attached). In any case, the expedition found gold in the Black Hills, and once the word was out it became impossible to stop the rush of white fortune-seekers. The government weakly gave way to this pressure and tore up the Indian treaty. In late 1875, at very short notice, all Indians were ordered to report to the reservation agency by 31 January 1876, a deadline which the Sioux could hardly have kept even if they had wanted to.

In *A Sharp Encounter* Charles Schreyvogel pictured what General Sherman called the 'vindictive earnestness' of the U.S. army's response to the Little Bighorn catastrophe. On many occasions entire Indian villages were destroyed and their people (including women and children) killed or taken into captivity.

The Sioux were not a gentle people. Their Indian enemies called them arrogant, ruthless trouble-makers. And now that they were at bay, with their sacred lands invaded, it was certain that they would make a stand. On 17 May 1875 the gaudy figure of Custer, his long fair locks cascading from under a wide-brimmed hat, and a blood-red scarf tied at the neck of his fringed buckskin shirt, led the 7th Cavalry on its familiar mission of punishing the Indians. In June, Sitting Bull was camped by the Little Bighorn, a tributary of the Yellowstone in southern Montana. He had with him those Indians of the northern plains who had refused to accept the system of the reservation: the Sioux sub-tribes of the Hunkpapa, the Brulé, the Minneconjou, and the Oglala, plus some Cheyenne and Blackfoot allies. In his rush for glory, Cluster foolishly dashed upon the waiting Indians without proper support. He and his regiment were wiped out to a man. The fight was over before one could 'light a pipe'. 'What did I do?' said Sitting Bull. 'Nothing. We did not go out of our country to kill them, they came to kill us and got killed themselves.'

The Last Rites

The battle at the Little Bighorn was a famous Indian victory, but it was only a fleeting success. If the free Indians prospered, then the U.S. government's entire system of agencies and reservations would totter. And if that happened, so Washington thought, then the ungovernable white demand for western lands and resources would exterminate the Indians entirely. The Indians had to be broken of their 'habits' – that is, the very foundations of their culture and forced on to reservations; and a vengeful Army gladly undertook this task. All over the north-west, there was a brief flare of despairing resistance. The Modocs of the Pacific coast broke out and killed two commissioners sent to deal with them. They were subdued, their leader 'Captain Jack' and three lieutenants were hanged, and the tribe was transported thousands of miles to Indian Territory. Then the Nez Percés, the old favourites of the mountain men, took up the struggle when they were ordered to a small reservation at Fort Lapwai in Idaho. Led by the intelligent and gallant Chief Joseph, the tribe ran rings round the Army for a couple of years until fatigue and hopelessness forced them to surrender.

Sitting Bull and the rebellious Sioux had been chased north of the border into Canada, and there, in October 1877, the fleeing remnants of the Nez Percés joined him. They were all beaten, and they knew it. 'Have pity on me,' Sitting Bull pleaded. 'My heart was made strong but now it is weak, and that is why the Americans want to lick my blood.' Even in Canada there was not enough room for them, and slowly the refugees drifted back to the disgrace and idleness of the reservation.

The last rites were written, in south and north,

by two of the fiercest and angriest of the Indian tribes: the Apache and the Sioux. Since the days of the Spaniards, the Apache in the South-West had hated and fought the white man. Under the warrior Cochise, a powerful band of Apaches had held off the U.S. Army until, in 1872, still undefeated, they had accepted a large reservation in their own wild, dry, and broken country. In 1877 the government tried to force all Apaches onto one central reservation in Arizona which was already being nibbled at by mineral prospectors. In 1881, the Apache erupted. Led by the great warrior Geronimo they fought for five years until, as with the Nez Percés, they conceded their hopeless cause. The warriors were dispersed far from their ancestral lands, many to Florida; Geronimo was taken to Oklahoma where he lived for 14 years as a sad relic of a once-free people.

Appropriately, the last curtain was drawn down by the Sioux. Sitting Bull and his followers had

Henry F. Farny's *Song of the Talking Wire* contrasts the apparent simplicity of the life of a Sioux hunter with the trappings of civilisation, represented by the overland telegraph. In fact, the telegraph became an important weapon against hostile Indians, for it enabled isolated communities and the U.S. army to give or receive advance warning of Indian tribes on the warpath.

straggled back from Canada in 1883 and lived on government hand-outs, unhappily confined on the northern reservations in Dakota. Then, around 1889, there were whispers of a revivalist Indian religion based on visions seen in Nevada by a Paiute brave. In the cult of the Ghost Dance the downtrodden Indians prepared for a salvation that would sweep the whites from the earth and allow the Indians to repossess their old lands. Rumours of this revelation frightened the whites. Indians on the reservations, normally dejected to the point of apathy, became excited and troubled. Gatherings were forming, strange promises were in the air. In 1890 government authorities mustered their forces to put down any rebellion. Sitting Bull, now elderly and aloof, was marked out as a figure likely to attract troublemakers. The Hunkpapa chief scented death, and said the larks had warned him of it.

In December the agency police, made up of tamed Indians but backed by U.S. soldiers, came to remove Sitting Bull from the reservation and take him to a military gaol. As he stepped outside, firing broke out. He was shot dead 'while resisting arrest' – killed, like so many prophets and saviours, by his own countrymen. Within two weeks the long-feared uprising of the Sioux took place. On the snowy banks of Wounded Knee Creek (a few miles north of the Nebraska-South Dakota line), Chief Big Foot and his Sioux braves put on the magic shirts of the Ghost Dance cult and struck back at the soldiers who had come to disarm them. It was a sharp, bloody tussle in the frozen wastes. Big Foot and some 150 Indians were killed, and Army losses were also heavy.

That was the end. Not even the supernatural power of the Ghost Dance could save the Indians. In despair, those who had been, but a short time before, the free-running lords of the Great Plains, retreated to the shame and poverty and alcoholism of the reservation.

The End of the Frontier

*By the last decade of the 19th century the
western states had become fully integrated with
the life of the nation as a whole. But
memories of the Old West remained fresh and
would soon become the stuff of
legend and romance....*

In 1890 the Superintendent of the U.S. Census Bureau declared that the frontier was closed. The westward movement had pushed the American boundary to its natural limit at the Pacific Ocean, and the land behind was filling up. In the 20 years before 1890 the population of the Dakotas, in the north, had increased from 14,000 to 500,000; in the south, the population of the Kansas territory in the same period increased from 364,000 to just under 1,500,000. In a land so vast these were still fairly thin numbers, but the old pattern of western development was no longer possible. Free land was now hard to come by. A man who packed up home and goods and wandered off to a new patch of ground was likely, in the 1890s, to be treading on some other person's rights and property. The roving pioneer, in the first days of the West, moved according to whim and had a licence to do as he pleased. The people of the West in 1890, settled into communities and tied down by the usual demands and business of civilised society, called for laws not licence.

Everything had happened so quickly. 'A nation is being born in a day,' the moralists complained in 1835, and they feared that this was a nation of wild men in the West, without government or order. 'What,' they lamented, 'will become of the West?' Ninety years of random, hectic development had been spurred on by a race of energetic individualists, eager to grab what they could, and not too fussy about how they got it. To the more sensitive members of the east coast establishment, they appeared crude and unruly.

Without doubt the frontier had always been a restless place, where the wilder spirits jostled with fortune and chanced their lives on luck and boldness. They gambled with fate just as they gambled with money, and their excesses at the tables mirrored their unstable lives. In Virginia City (Nevada) at the height of the silver boom, 'enormous piles of silver weighed down the tables, and frequently 10,000 dollars changed hands in a minute'. The rancher Joe Timberlake was seen to play with 1000-dollar chips. A visitor to Denver wrote in 1859, 'I saw the Probate Judge of the county lose 30 Denver lots in less than ten minutes, at cards, in the Denver House on Sunday morning, and afterwards observed the county sheriff pawning his revolver for $20 to spend in betting at faro'. In New Mexico Territory the governor bet – at gunpoint – his whole Territory against a Texas stockman who had wagered his ranch and 10,000 head of cattle.

The play of fortune was the essence of western life. Boom and bust: that was a very ordinary expectation which raised no eyebrows. Cities, towns, mines, ranches, businesses, partnerships, all swept in with a blare of trumpets, and often vanished with hardly a whimper. Henry Comstock, after whom the great Lode was named, found two Irish prospectors on Mount Davidson (Nevada)

with some curious blue dirt. He conned his way into a partnership with them. He then sold his share for a quick 11,000 dollars and two donkeys, thereby doing himself out of millions in future profit: he had had a third share in a mountain of silver ore. In 1870 a penniless Comstock killed himself in Bozeman, Montana. The Big Four of the Central Pacific railroad, originally small-time traders, made many millions – and kept them. Horace Tabor, a grocer turned U.S. senator, made many millions and lost them, and his destitute wife, Baby Doe, froze to death in a cabin at the Matchless Mine. The owner of the Independence Mine, turfed out of a smart hotel for being improperly dressed, returned and bought the hotel for cash down, just to sack the snooty manager.

OPPOSITE The real West? Charles M. Russell's *Gunfight* was based on an actual incident and was painted in 1900 – but it looks as if it could have been taken from any number of Western movies of the past 50 years.

BELOW Remington's sketches, paintings, and sculptures also helped to fix the 20th century's idea of the old-time cowboy.

Four of the most notorious
outlaws in Western history:
seated, Jesse (left) and
Frank James; standing, Cole
(left) and Bob Younger.
Inset: a poster offering a
reward for the capture of the
James brothers in July 1881.

Rule of the Gun

In the midst of temptations of sudden wealth and sudden power, where the wheel of fate spun so fast and so erratically, life was often cheap and law hard to find. Distance and loneliness made men and women self-reliant. The only order was that they fashioned for themselves. The Colt or the Winchester gave swifter remedies than the circuit judge. The estimate of those who died violently in the West, in the 50 years or so after 1830, goes as high as 20,000. Fights with Indians, brigandage, mining rivalries and claim jumping, range wars, cattle rustling, the stockman's quarrel with settlers and sheep-herders led many to an early grave.

The West had more than its share of savages and murderers. Desperadoes of the Plummer Gang in Montana, the Opdyke Gang in Idaho, and the Coon Hole Gang in Utah looted and killed. Few frontier towns avoided a visit, at some time, by monsters like Tom Horn, Sam Brown, or Boone Helm. Helm, a member of the Plummer Gang, who was caught and hanged by vigilantes in 1864, admitted to murder and cannibalism. He had seen death in all its forms, he boasted on the gallows, and was not afraid to die. 'There's one gone to hell,' he cried as another desperado swung out on the end of a rope. 'Kick away, old fellow. I'll be in hell with you in a minute.'

With company like this a gun was handy, almost a necessity, in the West. The favoured weapon was Samuel Colt's invention, the single-action, six-shooter revolver. It was a great lump of metal, weighing 1 kg (2¼ lb) and with a 200 mm (8 in) barrel, but it became part of western formal wear, particularly among cowboys, whose lonely life on the range, threatened by Indians and rustlers, gave them a sense of danger. The cowboy slicked up for town was likely to 'go heeled', not so much for shooting (the heavy revolver was notoriously inaccurate and the ordinary cowboy was no sharpshooter), but more to make a manly show and to be a hit with the ladies. The westerner would use his gun if he had to; but then he liked to get in close and bide his time, preferably shooting his enemy in the back. The gun, when it was used, was an aid to survival, not an instrument of chivalry.

A man coming to California, said Bayard Taylor, when he rubbed shoulders and drank healths with the Forty-niners, 'could no more expect to retain his old nature unchanged, than he could retain in his lungs the air he had inhaled on the Atlantic shore'. The very activity of the place 'created a spirit of excitement which frequently led to dangerous excesses'. And the same was true throughout the western frontier.

This might seem to be a sure recipe for anarchy; yet, to the admiration of Taylor, these people showed – perhaps *because* of their very different origins – 'a disposition to maintain order and secure the rights of all'. A rough-and-ready justice applied; it was democratically agreed upon and firmly car-

Western hero? 'Wild Bill' Hickok, a card-playing marshal, was reluctant to engage in gunplay, at which he was fast but poor of aim. Later he became a professional gambler, and died in 1876 from a bullet in the back of his head.

Western hero? Wyatt Earp, a rough customer who resigned as deputy marshal of Dodge City when its citizens decided to clean up the cow town. In Tombstone (Arizona) he and his brothers killed the Clanton gang of rustlers in a carefully fixed fight at the OK Corral. Earp died of old age in 1929.

ried out. It might lack dignity, however. Taylor witnessed, in Stockton, two men tied to a tree and publicly whipped for attempted rape, while the bystanders jeered and hooted at each blow. But it worked surprisingly well. In a huge territory, inhabited by so many ruffians, with no government, few rules, no police, hardly a lock or a bolt, and temptations that might undo a saint, somehow public order and safety were generally maintained. 'The capacity of a people for self-government,' Taylor proudly proclaimed, 'was never so triumphantly illustrated.' It gave the lie to the haughtily cynical conservative autocrats of the east coast who thought that western man was a beast to be avoided, chained, or caged.

By 1890 or thereabouts the local talent for self-government had got a grip on the old lawlessness. Western communities were by now no more dangerous than those in the East, and many claimed that, because of their history of mixed nationalities and equal opportunities, they were far more comradely and democratic. But the necessity for order was, in a sense, a denial of the western spirit. Peace and a respectable quietness checked the free, disorderly creativity of the western pioneer. Bayard Taylor thought that the chief characteristic of the emigrant to the frontier was 'an increase of activity, and proportionately, of reckless and daring spirit'. In these circumstances a man made something of himself – or he might starve. 'It was curious' Taylor continued, 'to see how men, hitherto noted for their prudence and caution, took sudden leave of those qualities, to all appearance, yet only prospered the more thereby.' That was how the ideal westerner saw himself: a person of boundless energy and enterprise, unconstrained, self-reliant. But by the 1890s he had become instead an ordinary worried citizen, with a head full of school-board meetings, watch committees, and tramway schedules.

In most societies the slow passage of time makes up for a past and fading age. But in the American West it all happened so quickly, and men could not forget it so easily. As one observer put it: 'A boy old enough to drive a chuck wagon with the first herd of long-horns entrained at Abilene could have seen the rise and fall of the kingdom and still have been no more than middle-aged when it lapsed into legend'. Geronimo, that archetypal image of Indian courage and resourceful ferocity, whose name brought fear to the old cavalryman's heart, died quietly in Oklahoma in 1909. Charles Goodnight, whom some called the first and the greatest of the cattlemen, lived until 1929, a 93-year-old who had opened and closed a whole period of western history.

Myth and Legend

As order and legislation came in to the West, and men saw the wild old days receding into the dustbin of the past, so they invented an instant legend out of their nostalgia, to keep alive and to praise the old spirit. Many of the myths were consciously created. Well-known western names, several of them with very dubious histories, were dusted off and given an imaginative polish by dime-novel writers and by such industrious publishers as Beadle & Adams. Pioneers like Daniel Boone, Army scouts like Kit Carson, buffalo hunters like William F. Cody, lawmen like Hickok and Wyatt Earp, gunmen like Billy the Kid, frontier trollops like Martha 'Calamity Jane' Cannaray, were all raised to heroic status. Re-created on the printed page in pulp magazines and cheap novels, they have had a new lease of life in the 20th century from film and television.

Art is never slow to alter and invent, but the western myth made some extraordinary portraits out of real lives. Wild Bill Hickok, ex-Pony Express man, ex-Union scout, first came to notoriety when he cut down his enemy David McCanles by lying in wait and shooting him from behind a curtain; the jury at his trial judged this killing to be in self-defence. In 1871 Hickok got the job of marshal in the raw new cattle town of Abilene (Kansas). He was a colourful addition to the town, with his fancy clothes and long wavy hair, but he did not last. He supervised his territory from a card table in the Alamo Saloon. When he was reluctantly drawn outside, his gun-play proved fast but a danger to friend as well as foe. Before the end of the summer he had shot his deputy by mistake, and was out of a job. He drifted north, joined Buffalo Bill's Wild West show, then married the proprietress of a rival outfit. In 1876 he was back on the frontier, in the gold-boom town of Deadwood, South Dakota, where he set up as a professional gambler with Calamity Jane by his side.

She was a frowsy, debauched alcoholic who had hob-nobbed with mule-skinners and rail-construction crews, and boasted of never going to bed sober. The gambler and his slattern did not have long to enjoy Deadwood. Cross-eyed Jack McCall shot Wild Bill through the back of the head, for a reason that was never discovered.

Hickok was not the only shady lawman to enter into legend: as we have seen (Chapter 5), Wyatt Earp's term as Wichita (Kansas) deputy marshal ended with his arrest for disorderly conduct. Earp and his friend Bat Masterson followed the cattle trains – they were both ex-buffalo hunters – and moved westward along the railroad to Dodge City, where Earp became assistant marshal and Masterson sheriff. They managed to combine their law duties with the more profitable task of running the faro game in the Long Branch Saloon. Masterson also had his own brush with the law; he was once fined 8 dollars for shooting a man through the lung. Around 1880 the citizens of Dodge decided to clean up their town, so Wyatt joined his brothers in Tombstone, a rough mining outpost in the Arizona desert. 'Doc' Holliday, the elegant but consumptive gambling dentist, found his way there too.

In this wild territory the Earp brothers and Holliday came into collision with the Clanton gang of cattle rustlers. In October 1881 they provoked the unprepared rustlers into a quarrel, and despatched them without compunction at the OK Corral, on the edge of town. Soon afterwards Virgil Earp, town marshal and gunman, was himself crippled by gunfire; and in 1882 his brother Morgan was shot dead in a pool-room. Wyatt Earp, Masterson, and Holliday retreated to Denver, where Doc Holliday

BELOW One of the nastiest killers in the West, William Bonney, alias Billy the Kid, shot more than 20 men before he, too, was killed by a lawman at the age of 22.

BELOW, LEFT A Colt 44.40 double-action revolver made in 1878. It was reputedly owned by C.L. 'Gunplay' Maxwell, a member of Butch Cassidy's Wild Bunch gang.

later died in a sanatorium and the other two went back to their old business at the faro tables. Masterson died in 1921, having become a sports writer on the New York *Morning Telegraph*. Earp retired to Los Angeles, where he lasted till 1929.

A fanciful invention made legends out of these tawdry lives. But what perverse talent turned stunted maniac William Bonney into Billy the Kid, steely-eyed badman and ace sharpshooter of the West? Within days of his death, in July 1881, Billy had entered popular literature as 'the outlaw who killed a man for every year of his life'. And the person who did most to promote him as an evil genius was his killer, Sheriff Pat Garrett.

The facts about William Bonney are in some doubt, but it seems that he was born in New York and taken to Santa Fe by his mother at a young age. He grew up an undersized, scrawny youth who got into bad company. By the age of 12 he had killed his first man, or so it was said. In 1876 he was in Arizona, in that dry, remote country which was the last wild frontier in the West. He was 18 and still a half-pint, but with a Colt 45 in his hand he reckoned himself the equal of any man. Naturally drawn to trouble, he got involved in the Lincoln County War in New Mexico where the cattle baron John Chisum was trying to run his animals over the rights of homesteaders and settlers. Billy the Kid began on the settlers' side, but was soon attracted away by the larger rewards offered by the richer cattlemen.

The hard and dangerous days of frontier life were over when 'Buffalo Bill' Cody's Wild West show toured America and Europe from the mid-1880s. His company of rough-riders, crack-shots, cowboys, and Indians was the first to cash in on a nostalgia for what outsiders imagined to have been the romance of the Old West.

BUFFALO BILL'S WILD WEST·
CONGRESS, ROUGH RIDERS OF THE WORLD.

MISS ANNIE OAKLEY,
THE PEERLESS LADY WING-SHOT.

There were several fights and ambushes, and men were killed. Billy did his share of the shooting, and perhaps he fired some of the fatal bullets; no one knows for certain. In any case, when an amnesty was declared Billy was on parole in Lincoln, under indictment for killing a law officer. He offered to turn state evidence, but jumped bail instead and fled to Fort Sumner, 160 km (100 miles) to the north.

Pat Garrett, newly-elected sheriff of Lincoln county, swore he would bring Billy back, and took horse for Fort Sumner also. After misadventures and shootings on the way, the sheriff closed in on Billy and his girlfriend. Then chance brought hunter and hunted, unbeknown to each other, to the same ranch-house. Garrett learned of his quarry's presence and, making no mistake, shot Billy from a bedroom window before the 22-year-old gunman could draw or defend himself. A sordid execution brought an end to a short, sordid life.

The Enduring Romance

The transformation of rogues into heroes was an innocent pastime that gave amusement to many and profit to a few. But the legends created by the dime novelists and acted out in the Wild West shows of Buffalo Bill and other smart managers of western make-believe had a more serious purpose, too. They celebrated, in a simple colourful form, the frontier virtues and reminded solid citizens that their safe, orderly existence perhaps missed out on some important aspects of life. The myths omitted the filth, danger, and meanness of the frontier and sang instead of energy, endurance, loyalty, and idealism. 'I wish I could find words to express,' cattleman Charles Goodnight wrote, 'the trueness, the bravery, the hardihood, the sense of honour, the loyalty to their trust and to each other of the old trail hands.' Bayard Taylor saw the Americans of the West as a kind of modern Viking – passionate people, full of rage and power and daring. 'Those who retained their health,' Taylor wrote, 'seemed to revel in an exuberance of animal spirits, which carried them over barriers and obstacles that would have brought others to a full stand.'

Those days were now gone, but a young nation with much to do in the world wanted to believe in them. The people wanted to applaud their past. When, in 1885, Buffalo Bill persuaded Sitting Bull to leave the boredom of the reservation and join his Wild West Show, the audience hissed the Sioux chief for killing Custer, but cheered him and pressed money on him for being the magnificent enemy in the noble American game of Cowboys and Indians. Sitting Bull was not deceived. 'The tipee is a better place,' he said, resigning from the show after one season. 'I am sick of the houses and the noises and the multitude of men.' The Indian chief was one American, at least, who still preferred reality to make-believe.

But the rest of America – other than the dispossessed Indians – yearned for the past, for the democratic and libertarian virtues of western individualism, and for the discipline and awe inspired by the fast-vanishing wilderness. The poet Walt Whitman, writing nostalgic hymns to his country's greatness, saw the West as 'the real genuine America'. And sober historians agreed. 'The West,' one wrote, 'is the most American part of America.' Something great, and characteristically American, had been achieved in the West. By 1900 the prophetic boast made by the historian Henry Adams had largely come true: 'Look at my wealth! See these solid mountains of salt and iron, of lead, copper, silver, and gold. See these magnificent cities scattered broadcast to the Pacific! See my cornfields rustling and waving in the summer breeze. Look at this continent of mine, fairest of created worlds'.

In the popular view the westward movement was the well-spring from which America drew its finest qualities. 'The one grand lesson of the settlement and organization of the country,' Bayard Taylor wrote from California in 1849, 'is of a character that ennobles the race'. A gigantic energy and resourcefulness were turned to great ends. 'The unanimity with which all united,' Taylor continued, 'the frankness with which the old prejudices of sect and party were disclaimed, the freshly awakened pride of country, formed a spectacle which must claim our entire admiration.'

Some later critics were not so admiring. They saw an aggressive movement advancing in squalor, greed, and violence. They saw native Indians tricked and bullied and hunted almost to the point of extinction. They saw a virgin land despoiled, numberless buffaloes slaughtered, hills deforested, mountains ripped open and mine-tailings scattered like confetti. They saw mine owners, railroad promoters, cattle corporations growing fat on fraud, exploitation, and oppression. They saw the dregs of many nations sowing the West with disease, alcoholism, treachery, and sudden death. They saw the rule of the gun and lynch-law.

There is room for both views of the American West. It was a place of idealism, and a country of the bad and selfish. The history of a nation is a complex story, with many strands woven into the tapestry. But what stands out with startling clarity, what appeals even now to film-makers just as it appealed to Bayard Taylor in 1850 and to cheap novelists in 1890, is the grandeur of man or woman alone, tested in the adversity of the wilderness and winning through in triumph. That was what the old cowboy Jim McCauley was saying, with poor grammar and shaky spelling but with moving sincerity, when he wrote of 'the wild free life whare you have to feel if your closest friend is still on your hip, and if your old horse will make it in, and to make the Mexico line and get back without any holes in your hide – that is real living . . . but 'tis the violent kind and lots of people love it beyond a doubt'.

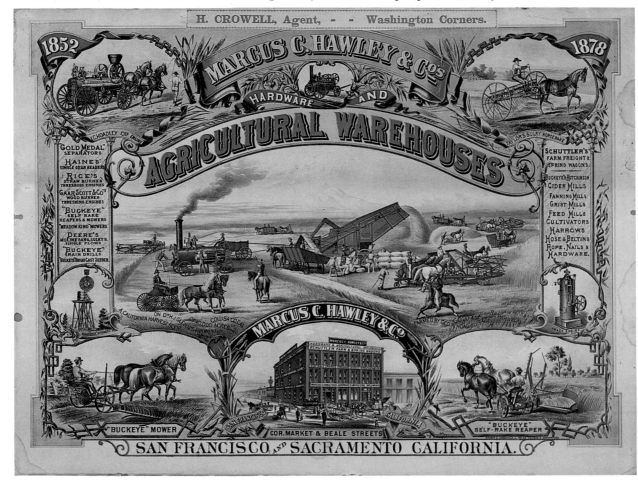

The western landscape was well on the way to becoming domesticated when this advertisement appeared in 1878. The farmers were ploughing the soil and harvesting their crops with steam-powered machinery made in western factories. The frontier of the wilderness, which had retreated westward throughout the 19th century, had finally vanished.

Index

Page numbers in *italics* refer to picture captions.

Acknowledgements

The publishers thank the following organisations and individuals for their kind permission to reproduce the pictures in this book:

Aldus Archive (British Museum) 10, (British Museum Newspapers Library) 14-15; Courtesy Amon Carter Museum, Fort Worth 12, 46, 48, 61, 64-5, 66-7; The Anschutz Collection/James O. Milmoe endpapers, half-title, 26, 52, 63, 69; Arizona State Historical Society 77 right; Buffalo Bill Historical Centre 23; California Historical Society 35; Denver Art Museum 70-1; Denver Public Library, Western History Department 11, 51, 76 above; Kansas State Historical Society 21, 48-9; Library of Congress/Orbis Library 74-5; Metropolitan Museum of Art, Morris K. Jesup Fund, 1933 17; National Museum of Art, Smithsonian Institute 4-5, (Gift of Mrs Joseph Harrison, Jr) 24, 41; Nebraska Historical Society 30-1; New Hampshire Historical Society 56-7; New York Public Library, I.N. Phelps Stokes Collection; Astor, Lenox and Tilden Foundation 34; Art Department, The Oakland Museum 36-7; Oregon Historical Society 16; Peter Newark's Western Americana 20, 32-3, 40, 42, 43, 44, 47, 53, 62, 66, 72, 73, 77 left, 78; Public Archives of Canada 13; Robin May Collection 74 (inset); St Johnsbury Athenaeum Inc. 2; St Louis Art Museum, Gift of Mr J. Lionberger Davis, St Louis, Mo. 28-9; Courtesy of The Shelburne Museum, Shelburne 19; Southern Pacific Railways 58-9; Southwest Museum, Los Angeles 68 inset; The Thomas Gilcrease Institute of American History and Art, Tulsa, Oklahoma 38, 54-5; Union Pacific Railway 60-1; Department of Special Collections, University of California 79; U.S. Forest Service 57 inset; U.S. National Archives 76 below; Washington University Gallery of Art, St Louis 8-9; Whitney Gallery of Art, Cody, Wyoming 68; William Rockhill Nelson Gallery of Art, Kansas City, Mo. 2-3.